The Branding Book

The Secrets of Personal Branding Success.

By

Mark Lewis

The Branding Book is subject to Copyright law.

Mark Lewis
The Branding Book

© 2014, Mark Lewis
Lulu Press (first edition).
thebrandingbook@gmail.com

ISBN 978-1-291-65854-5

Contents

**Visit www.thebrandingbook.co.uk for
updates, extra content and more!**

First Edition – December 2013.

PREFACE

Social media and viral news have prompted a new perspective on how we represent ourselves to the rest of the world. The possibilities have become almost infinite. Waiting on an 'opportunity to knock' has become a secondary notion. You could use Facebook just to keep in touch with your old school friends, or you could make use of its various facilities to be vocal about what you have to offer the rest of the world both professionally and personally right now.

Business ventures or a new outlook on life and professional advancement have all taken the face of social media interactions and turned them into something more evolved. This is where the introduction of this book lies. Personal branding in itself is not a new concept as this book will illustrate. It's a conscious choice to educate the rest of the world and show them what you are all about. The emergence of online marketing tools have just made it more convenient and raised the bar because with ease of communication and common motives comes competition. Lots of it. So, your best bet is to be the better brand out there in a sea of brands swimming against the tide and trying to get noticed.

This book will guide someone who is looking for an in depth view of the online world of personal branding. The elements that make personal branding what it is and what you as a personal brand are made up of. This will not only show you your weaknesses, but it will help you realize more of your strengths and how to capitalize on them through online resources which are not just limited to Facebook and twitter.

Thanks to the continuous evolution of both communicational and vocational technology, job profiles and expectations have been changing to suit the new career paradigm. Achieving a personal brand status, which not only introduces your message to the world, but also gets you a response in the form of better professional and personal relationships is something this book encompasses on a whole new level. Inspirational stories of successful personal brands might have that slight cheese factor, but a good uplifting story always motivates the human psyche. Stories and anecdotes are memorable and stick in the mind much better than any statistic ever could. Most books only talk about the potential of success and its ramifications on the rest of your life, but this book will also talk about failure and how it is just as important in shaping and molding your perfect personal branding image. A real brand image is made up of failure and successful achievement. Some would argue that you cannot get a brand image without some type of failure – everyone likes an underdog who overcomes obstacles to become better than the mainstream. Apple, for example, is a prime example of this, as is Google. However errors in terms of personal branding can be a lot more damaging than 'not being the cutting edge'. Mistakes in the age of semi permanent internet records are something inevitable, but this book will shine a light on not only the common mistakes, but those small niggling doubts we all have when we try to turn our Facebook or Linked In profile into the state of the art testament to your carefully crafted self image.

The majority of branding books will stop at this and decide that once you are successful that's all that matters. You have been given your instructions, they say, now go out and put them to good use. Well, it does matter, but that's not where this book ends. Successful personal brands are always reinventing themselves. Innovation is the mother of all opportunities. Think Madonna, who has constantly and consistently reinvented herself and her image over the years and has subsequently even more successful now than she was in the earlier years. This book will talk about reinventing brands after a successful run and response from your public and it will talk about the very aspects of personal branding blue print that all of us desperately want to be privy to. Whatever your story is, superimpose the blue print over it to elevate your story from ordinary to something that attracts an audience that will appreciate you and your brand and it will open all those doors you have been trying hard to reach for your entire life.

This book is about improving your online image and creating a brand new you. Use the following skills wisely and learn how to adapt your image in today's constantly competitive society.

INTRODUCTION TO PERSONAL BRANDING

"Personal branding is about managing your name — even if you don't own a business — in a world of misinformation, disinformation, and semi-permanent Google records. Going on a date? Chances are that your "blind" date has Googled your name. Going to a job interview? Ditto."

- Tim Ferriss, Author of the 4-Hour Work Week

Image managing, a term synonymous with personal branding is something that has been coming up in the media quite a lot lately and is no doubt considered an invaluable source of communication with the rest of the world. An ongoing, atomic internet revolution later we stand at the brink of a new frontier, the frontier of personal brand development. This personal brand paradigm shift is that literally defines your personal and professional image to the rest of the world.

How did image revolution come about? And what are the implications of the revolution on your career?

Referring to Tim Ferris's quote, it is amazing, the power a web browser holds in its many complex layers of mass information. A prospective employer can look you up online and view your working history. Seems like a whole lot of hoopla that online clout might be a working catalyst that gets you a job?

Get out of here!

Clout might have seemed significant only on paper, like your well built and carefully crafted resume, but in this internet aware age, most companies require you to fill details of your resume on their online profiles. Clout can be evasive in many undefined ways, especially if you don't know how to go about maintaining it once you've started crafting an image, but one thing is for sure. Clout is sure get you noticed, and it set's you apart from the vastly available competition.

History of personal branding

Social media and web applications, which support professional connections, might be new, but personal branding itself is not a new concept. In fact, personal branding goes as far back as 1937.

"What the mind of man can conceive and believe, it can achieve."

The hallmark expression of an American author, Napoleon Hill, who broached the subject of personal branding in his bestselling book called, *'Think and Grow Rich'*. His book talked about self positioning, or branding and how they helped churn out personal success for a person. He believed in having firm beliefs and knowing what direction you wanted your life to take. According to his philosophy, most people had no clear beliefs, and this is why success was highly improbable for them. His book sold over 20 million copies, and to this date continues to be a best seller.

The idea of self positioning was broached again in 1981 with Al Reis and Jack Trout's book, *'Positioning – The battle for you mind'*. The books key principle being, *'don't try to do everything yourself. Find a horse to ride.'* The horse being a paradigm for whatever means you use to position yourself in a market. In today's world that constitutes the World Wide Web. A few decades ago it was networking at office parties and drinks at the club or carefully placed - and carefully worded - advertisements in the local newspaper.

Since we are talking about the history of personal branding, the initiation, or launch of this idea is much better explained through the shift of employer-employee relationship perspective and traditional concepts of our professional identity than just the internet's auspicious arrival into our lives and books on personal success.

The downsizing, merging, and laying off of employees in reputable multinational companies about forty years ago created a rift in the image carved out by the employers industry. The general purpose of which was to promise millions of employees job security for life. The wrongful assumptions of lifelong economic stability had finally started to transform into stronger survival tactics to steer their own vocational destinies in the right direction.

As experts in career progress and job hunting started challenging the traditional view of work, previously considered a social responsibility, which is meant to be a burden. Personal job satisfaction emerged as the new mantra every human resource manager started to specialize in. Once the work culture started changing through the interconnected network of employees, hiring experts and employers a semi defined picture of self promotion and positioning start to emerge. The internet is merely the tool that brought about the emancipation in professional and private network creation and has thrust the reigns of your own vocational destiny into your hands. You no longer need to rely on someone else to create a likeable image of you, or maintain it for you. That job has fallen to the person themselves. This is both an opportunity and a risk. If you know how to do well out of it, you can be vastly ahead of the game in multiple domains.

Don't worry though; this isn't a corporate specific book. We are merely discussing the job industry as a way to look deeper into the development of personal branding and how it really came to be. As Tim Ferris stated, personal branding is not just about getting a job, it's so much more than an intangible replacement of job security. Your personal image, online can affect you in life changing ways that you weren't aware of. We will take a look at all those benefits in the coming chapters. For now let's glide back to what personal branding really means to you and to everyone you meet.

CHAPTER 1 – WHAT IS PERSONAL BRANDING ABOUT?

As I discussed earlier, personal branding is all about careful craftsmanship, of your image and the way in which you present yourself to the public. Think of yourself as a product who is trying to become an established brand, to be purchased or acquired by everyone. The way you market yourself both online and offline will bring you recognition and generate interest beyond a simple, cleverly crafted sophisticated resume, or slightly complex resume. Sir Alan Sugar and Oprah Winfery aren't the only ones that can create a brand. These days anyone with a connection to the rest of the world, i.e. is online has the tools to create a 'brand' for themselves, in order to promote themselves and stand out from the crowd.

Personal branding opens doors that were previously unknown and unavailable to you. The metaphorical limited peripheral vision you might have allowed yourself to have whist not making use of the internet's many astounding resources will soon become one of those stories that you can tell at parties about how you didn't know what you were missing out on.

1. Defining your Identity

Personal branding is about defining your own identity to yourself before launching it to the viewer. Know who you are, personally, and professionally. Place yourself in a market segment that you know that will care about who you are, or will want your professional connection as a part of their vast network, something that can propel you towards greater success, but before you can go for self representation in any form, you need to be aware of your current self image and what you have to offer. Unless you know where you stand you won't be able to figure out the path ahead.

2. Who are you?

As a brand, who do you hope to be and what do you hope to be? A professional statement or a personal one? Why are you building a personal brand? These are questions you should ask yourself before you can begin your personal branding journey. Things will go much smoother if you know your direction.

3. Elements of Personal Branding

Personal branding is made up of several important elements, without them your brand won't be particularly authentic. And for a brand to be successful, it needs to be authentic in the sense that it needs to have its own uniqueness which reflects heavily on the image you want to build.

So, Remember (Professor Hubert Rampersad, 2008) says:

No vision + no self-knowledge + no self-learning + no thinking + no mindset change + no integrity + no happiness + no passion + no sharing + no trust + no love

= no authentic Personal Branding

---

4. Your Story

Everyone wants to know how you came from point A to point B, and what you did to get there. A great story always attracts others to you and your cause. The expertise that you hold in your niche and how you came about to achieve this knowledge, all the stumbles and hurdles along the way make for an irresistible charm that attracts support and interest from others because people love a good underdog to success story.

One example of a successful story is football player Lewis Howes. He's an American, former professional football player who is listed as one of 'five internet guru's that can make you rich', and is one of the '50 most influential people in blogging'. Recently, he was recognized by president Obama as one of the top 100 entrepreneurs in the country who is under 30.

"Lewis has a heart of gold. His story is extremely inspirational and his willingness to help others is like so few people."

— Noah Kagan, CEO at AppSumo.com

Due to an injury sustained while playing, he underwent corrective surgery and later ended his football career. However, since then he has built several successful multimillion dollar online businesses, and remains and inspiration to all other young aspiring entrepreneurs. His story exudes a certain impressive charm, everything the public loves about a man who takes a fall and comes back stronger is more attractive than a just a prolonged football career in which he has already excelled as well.

5. Your Voice

There are many things that can be said about 'finding your voice' in this process and conveying a message that others would want to wholeheartedly accept as a strong and authentic message. A lot of us misunderstand this. We assume personal branding allows us to muffle our real voice and come up with a different voice, an image that has very little do with our selves.

The real deal here is, be natural.

Communicate with the world personal branding wise as if you were talking to a friend, face to face. You should focus on translating your real life voice into great content, no matter what format you use for it. It could be just a blog post, or it could be a speaking engagement, Facebook even, tweet, or a podcast. If you try to act like someone else then you are only going to look fake and people are always astute at assessing the fakers from the authentic. So, make sure your 'voice' is authentic and not some imitation.

Be clear about your message and just try to use simple language. If you try to use fillers people are going to think you are just trying to be overtly smart and your message won't get across because the target audience will get distracted.

Try to create value by communicating your own point of view on something to your audience instead of copying what others say and sounding the same really. Your uniqueness regarding a perspective is the one that will bring you more success. People like hearing a different point of view from the sea of conformity.

6. Your packaging

How are you visually connecting with the target audience? This holds as much importance as any other point in this topic. How you visually define your personal brand to other goes a long way in ensuring that others remember you and find your brand captivating. Of course the content is much more important that the color of your blog site, but is not to say that it's unimportant. In fact, it's a known fact that certain colors can attract and repel users from a website. Certain warm colors are more inviting and certain colors and images correspond with a brand image better than you can imagine.

Do your research, find out what colors attractive to the general user, and maybe take a look around at your competition to get some inspiration. Remember being unique and one of a kind gives you an edge above others, at the very least it attracts audience your way to some percentage and when you start with personal branding, every little helps.

7. Your transparency

While it is true that when you are trying to create a personal brand you may come to believe at some point a certain image is important to keep you afloat and your audience interested, but as I said before a posed performance is easy to spot. Don't be fake or robotic because people like a real person beneath the layers of World Wide Web, they don't like a robot.

There should be a balance in the way you show your transparency though. Have a well balanced approach when it comes to both transparency and privacy. Know what facets of your life you would like to keep private from others and how transparent you want to be for your audience.

Mistakes are a part of life and we should always take lessons from a heartfelt mistake. Nevertheless social media will amplify that message so be careful of what you're putting out there and take advantage of social media to withdraw, or apologize for a mistake.

8. Your Online Platform

How are you going to connect with the rest of the world and communicate your message? You need an online platform such as a blog website, YouTube account, Facebook profile, etc. Don't just join up every social network and hope for the best results. Think about how you want to portray your message and what platforms will best present your message to others. Strategize your personal branding success in an intelligent manner and leave a trail that is lasting on the World Wide Web.

Think of these online platforms as a stage to deliver your message to the target audience. What do you want them to know about you and how do you want to interact with them. Consider the pros and cons of joining Linked in, Facebook, and Twitter together. Platforms that complement each other will make a good choice and will help you in brand personal brand development.

Once you're into all of this, get more technical with word press providers and bandwidths. If you've planning webinars on YouTube look into what kind of camera you want to use and what subjects you want to introduce. Plan your blog posts accordingly and interact with your audience via all these platforms.

9. Your Self-Marketing

This is also the most important part of personal branding. If you have a message to deliver that is remarkable and you feel it will help others in some way, or form, then you should learn to market yourself properly to the masses. The world is a vast sea of diverse views and happenings. The way of communication has become of utmost importance. Just remember it has become far easier to offend someone overseas today than it was some decades ago.

Self promotion is not all about the 'me,me,me' syndrome. It is about displaying your attractive qualities, or displaying attributes that are important to others. 'OTHERS' is the key word here. You are defined by what others think of you as a personal brand. If you've worked with reputable clients, it's good to have a sort of 'social proof' every once in a while through good recommendations and testimonials.

It's just like when you have an online resume, Client testimonials on your blog will greatly improve and increase the job offers you receive. More people will sit up and take notice of your personal brand because you are preferred by well known clients.

10. Your Partnerships

Creating partnerships with influential brands will increase your own brands proclivity to be noticed, for example collaborations on e-books, webinars, etc. When looking to collaborate with someone take time research how influential the other brand is and how big of a community or following the person has. It would be ideal for you to find someone who is similar to you, or someone with a more established name would go a long way in increasing your clout. Partnering with someone of less presence online will only increase the other individual's chances.

We'll get out of the online world to illustrate an example and let's move to the entertainment industry:

Adam Levine = Superstar.

Christina Aguilera = Superstar.

Adam Levine + Christina Aguilera = Superstar Powerhouse (Moves like Jagger was a smash hit!).

11. Your Product

Digital products are hot commodities these days and they help with building a good reputation for you when you start on your personal branding journey. Writing a book, the kind that you can get on Barnes and Nobles can be great, but hard to get published in your first try. You would do better if you tried the many online platforms for self publishing. Blogging itself is a form of self published articles. Writing e-books and creating webinars and YouTube conferences is just another way to increase your brand recognition on the web.

You could try to self publishing and distributing as many copies as possible to others, but digital products like webinars and e-books sell more and give you a wider audience (more traffic on your website = more attention). You are able to find more

people interested in your message if you promote
your product in a way that appeals to others.

CHAPTER 2 - PERSONAL BRANDING IN THE MAKING - THE PERSONAL BRANDING BLUEPRINT

What makes a personal brand, personal and unique? Personal branding is not about being a celebrity it's about being able to get your message across to the right people and gaining recognition in the form of career furthering opportunities and relationships that are mutually beneficial. Passion and a derived purpose play an important role in making of a personal marketing; they are the foundation step of creating an image.

1. **Understanding oneself** - building self esteem.

Self learning is an important exercise in any walk of life really. Personal branding takes your understanding of oneself very seriously. A strong self confidence inspires interest on many fronts from brand viewers. So, start your journey of personal branding through learning about yourself as an individual. Unless you are sure of who are professionally and personally, you cannot create a strong image for yourself because your lack of self awareness will only show up as low self esteem, all of which will be reflected on the image you are trying to painstakingly create. Remember, image building and sharpening takes time, effort and patience. And all of these can be helpful once you've figured out your own place and develop a confident personality that shows up in the brand development stages. Always smile and put your confident side forward.

2. **Be yourself, others are already taken (Oscar Wilde) - The uniqueness, Individuality & existence.**

Another extraneously important factor for building a personal brand is to be yourself and maintain a uniqueness, which revolves around you and is not a revamped clone of someone else. Think brand differentiation, or USP (Unique selling point) and apply that yourself. Think of what will set you apart from the crowd. Marketing what aspect of you will appeal to a prospective employer? Emphasizing a unique characteristic of your personal brand is one of the reasons you will get recognized in your field.

It might be your experience, attitude, approach, or your philosophy that sets you apart from the myriads of competition. This could just as well simply be your personal style. The way you dress, your communication skills, how you're addressing people, your body language, and whether you make eye contact could also be the key in providing you with a competitive edge when it comes to high profile job interviews, where many different candidates with similar qualifications and experience are interviewed by a review panel.

Your Unique Selling Proposition is actually the result of developing your personal brand.

- Finding qualities that are unique within you and using those as guide posts.

- Define the purpose of your brand, by identifying your goals in this regard.

- Find out in what way can your personal brand benefit others.

Once you understand these points, you can get further in your path towards an authentic personal brand that is unique and demands attention from others.

3. Brand USP's

As Steve Jobs once said:

"You can't connect the dots looking forward; you can only connect them looking backwards. So you have to trust that the dots will somehow connect in your future. ... This approach has never let me down, and it has made all the difference in my life."

For most of us, learning your purpose can be an ongoing effort and it may involve your thought process evolving through it, just try to keep asking yourself:

- What am I unique at?

- What makes me feel like I'm valued?

- And am I betraying myself?

Asking yourself these three questions will bring you closer to realizing your dream of the purpose of your life. This will also bring you closer to realizing your brands unique selling point. Every brand small or big has one. Personal branding is no stranger to this concept.

Examples of some general and the some unusual USP's:

- Domino's unique selling point still stands at being able to deliver your pizza to you hot, in less than an hour, or they won't take money from you. Yes, that is the general expectation we have from all fast food services, but not all promise timely delivery, or money back guarantee. And especially since fast food is a time sensitive commodity, delays in delivery can almost certainly happen every now and then, but at least you won't lose your money on cold pizza and Domino's will not a lose a loyal customer. Now you must be getting a hang of what a unique selling point represents.

- L'Oreal Paris, is long revered as the affordable range of beauty products that provide you with good value for money that are great for the skin and hair. Their strategy is to promote the brand as a luxury product that the customer has every right to indulge in. 'L'Oreal, because you are worth it.' Is the ultimate, attractive resonance every woman viewer looks for in a cosmetic product and wants quality above all other factors like the price not being as expensive as other quality brand's. This does not negatively affect the image of the brand. Yet again a simple, but brilliant USP strategy has kept L'Oreal this long in the game.

- Now for a slightly unusual USP. UMMI couture. Sadaf Ahmad's a London based Designer whose main USP in the beginning collections were flattering maternity wear, which were not only beautiful prints and colors, but also fusion wear. She created a niche in the marketing segment for herself, which brought her countless customers and gave the new business an edge that new customers were quick to catch on.

4. Values - What values do you provide?

You always hear about values being the cornerstones of every company, or brand. So, what is all the song and dance about related to values? And how does it fuel your character?

Values are guideposts that you use to guide you with your decisions and in life, they are a driving force for your personal brand, and affect the brands success in a multitude of ways because your internal, intrinsic values are the one that are deeply rooted inside you and make you take a certain decision, or launch yourself with a certain image that helps you get noticed. Know your core values, as a personal brand. What are the values you would offer someone? Surprisingly, there is a big list of possible values that

can promote your personal brand. The list is courtesy
http://www.dummies.com.

Possible Values for Your Personal Brand

Abundance	Acceptance	Accomplishment
Accuracy	Achievement	Acknowledgment
Activeness	Adaptability	Adventure
Affection	Affluence	Agility
Altruism	Ambition	Appreciation
assertiveness	Attractiveness	Availability
Awareness	Balance	Beauty
being the best	Belonging	Boldness
Bravery	Brilliance	Calmness
Challenge	Charity	Charm
Clarity	Cleanliness	Comfort
commitment	Compassion	Completion

Composure	Concentration	Congruency
Connection	Consciousness	Consistency
Contentment	Contribution	Control
Coolness	Cooperation	Correctness
Courage	Creativity	Credibility
Curiosity	Daring	Decisiveness
Dependability	Determination	Devotion
Dignity	Diligence	Diplomacy
Discipline	Discovery	Diversity
Drive	Duty	Education
Effectiveness	Efficiency	Elegance
Empathy	Endurance	Energy
Enjoyment	Enthusiasm	Excellence
Excitement	Experience	Expertise
Expressiveness	Extroversion	Fairness

Faith	Fame	Family
Fearlessness	Fidelity	financial independence
Fitness	Flexibility	Focus
Freedom	Friendliness	Frugality
Fun	Generosity	Giving
Grace	Gratitude	Growth
Happiness	Harmony	Health
Helpfulness	Heroism	Honesty
Humility	Humour	Hygiene
Imagination	Independence	Insightfulness
Inspiration	Integrity	Intelligence
Intimacy	Introversion	Intuition
Joy	Justice	Kindness
Knowledge	Leadership	Learning

Liberty	Logic	Love
Loyalty	making a difference	Mastery
mindfulness	Motivation	Neatness
Obedience	open-mindedness	Optimism
organization	Originality	Passion
Peace	Perfection	Perseverance
philanthropy	Playfulness	Pleasantness
Pleasure	Polish	Popularity
Power	Practicality	Pragmatism
Precision	Preparedness	Privacy
Professionalism	Prosperity	Realism
Reason	Recognition	Recreation
Relaxation	Reliability	Resilience
Resourcefulness	Respect	Restraint

Sacrifice	Satisfaction	Security
self-control	Selflessness	self-reliance
Serenity	Service	Significance
Silence	Simplicity	Sincerity
Skilfulness	Solitude	Spirituality
Spontaneity	Stability	Strength
Success	Support	Sympathy
Synergy	Teamwork	Temperance
Traditionalism	Timeliness	Tranquillity
Trustworthiness	Truth	Understanding
Uniqueness	Variety	Victory
Virtue	Vision	Warmth
Wisdom		

Why not add two more in the spaces provided above?

You can use your newly founded or recognized values to build a short and snappy mission statement for your personal brand. You should be able to identify about 10 of basic values from this list, which is by no means complete. Additional, new values not featured here are also considered guiding principles that will bring your brand success.

5. Build a platform to connect

Once you're ready to implement your values and strengths, you need a platform to connect with your client base, or target market. Building platforms to connect with the rest of the world is easier than expected in today's internet savvy world.

You won't be at loss, of how many platforms exist to get your personal brand across, but you might get confused about how to integrate all these platforms in the best way to secure a consistent image of yourself online. The best online platforms for personal branding have existed for quite some time now. The trick is how to unify them in a way that will strengthen and support your brand identity.

Facebook: Facebook is more than just a platform for social connects, where you go to keep in touch with old friends, who have gotten scattered over a period of time. Facebook's intrinsic values consist of an application for easily forming connections with one another. You're Facebook page can be professional and private. Try to keep two separate profiles for the professional facet of your life. Bring your core values and strengths to your Facebook page.

Twitter: Twitter, a later development is the fastest connecting platform for authentic information updates. Once you have a certain amount of following on twitter, you can use it to your advantage. Once your brand is featured online in other platforms like Facebook, Linked In, and blogs, etc. twitter will keep you connected to your followers and who are aware of your presence as a personal brand and agree with your core values and what you have to offer.

LinkedIn: This is a professional platform foremost and links you're professionally to a network of work histories and online resumes. And somehow it's more than just all of this. A Linked In profile is looked up my more employers than we are generally aware. Most companies nowadays look at your Linked In profile before going into business with you, or even asking you for an interview.

This personal branding platform has changed the meaning of simple networking for careers. It strengthens and extends your contacts. The intrinsic values of linked in center around being connected, looked for and finding people with your professional interest, the career empowering comes afterwards and is one of the larger goals of the website, which it has been consequently been achieving since its establishment. It has connected over 225 million people worldwide professionally enabling them to all own and manage a certain personal brand. The way these three platforms unify to provide a more concise and refined view of your personal brand is the real key to success.

Blogging: A new age personal branding tool, which is just as reverent in molding and showing the world your image as a social network. You can use blogging as a way to share your values and establish a brand identity online. The blogging platform provides linking resources, which help with unifying your personal brand platforms together more cohesively.

Creating an image on blogging of yourself with a few keywords related to your expertise and knowledge will help lead people to you, but what will keep them interested is your consistent bios, a good elevator pitch and most important of all, original content. Create original content and become a leader in your industry through well placed pitches, aimed at the right target audience. All of this is a breeze once you have a proper direction planned for yourself. A confused brand identity won't connect with the audience as readily as a well thought out, confident blog identity because it greatly affects your personal branding process.

6. Customer Support – join the conversation

Customer support an important segment of every customer retailer/service provider relationship and it gives you a leg up on the competition. Customer service actively affects brand perception because the customer base expects your brand vision to be built around a customer service policy. This is something that has been referred to time and time again with brand promotion. A happy customer is a loyal customer. Personal branding suffers from immediate depth perception issues if you're not prepared to deal with customers properly.

Remember Domino's core values of timeliness and money back guarantee are built on the customer support relationship. Your personal brand should be much in the same way connected to the target audience's customer support expectations. So, take an initiative and proactively contact customers through the networks at your disposal. Send them good greetings, show some appreciation for their support and actively join the flow of comments on your content blog posts. Post newsletters to interactive customers and gain their support and trust.

7. Innovation

Being innovative again ties into your USP, whereas here you look for ways to create that distinction from others in the same field. Innovation is the key element which drives a brand forward and gets it noticed by more. Personal branding should be no different in this aspect. Innovation and inspiration translating through your established platforms will bring you unlimited success.

Always be on the lookout for innovation. Visualize where you want to be as a brand in the next few years and find inventive way to make that come about.

Adopt innovation as a success achieving, marketing pillar that is unavoidable because of changing ever changing technology. Actors like Felicia Day changed the image of nerds as computer geeks with quirky kinks in her web series called 'The Guild'. This was innovation on her part, developing a brand from scratch and innovating with the web series' evolution really brought a whole new level of popularity to a show that was just followed by a few hundred on YouTube. Brand marketing and innovative brand packaging has brought the show to the attention of more audiences.

CHAPTER 3 - THE TRADITIONAL CAREER PARADIGM – THE NEW REALITY

Let's be honest, most traditional paradigms for your lifestyle have become obsolete because of the increase in technology's intervention in our lives and because of the massive communication lines that have been opened up to us personally and professionally. There is no denying that the traditional career paradigm has been affected by all these means in different ways.

www.Careerfolk.com really puts it all in perspective when they say:

'Welcome to the new "work order". The career as we know it is dead. You may not realize it, but you just got promoted to BOSS, the boss of your career. And here's how to deal with it.'

1. What's Out Now: The Traditional Career.

What Is In Now: The Short-term/Multiple Careers/Multiple income stream Model.

- There was a time, particularly with the baby boomer generation, which generally stayed with one company for years and retired in their old age from the same company. Loyalty and diligent work characteristics were highly appreciated by companies and subsequently rewarded.

- With limited technological advancement companies were more or less stable and job security was a reliable assurance for employees who saw this as a certain degree of job satisfaction, but with time and changing organizational dynamics job security is stated, but can't be promised. Employees are looking to advance in careers further beyond a certain degree and are prepared to change companies after 2-3 years.

2. What is Out Now: Full-time Permanent Jobs.

What is In Now: Contract/Part-time/Consulting Work.

• We currently live in a freelance economy. Jobs are harder to hold on to then they were twenty years ago and job security is a term that is rarely brought up by employers because there is no telling when the next downsizing or laying off might come to pass. With crashing economies it's hard to promise someone a career in the same company for the foreseeable future. It would do you good to be a proactive agent and start looking at the state of economy and its implications before pursuing your prospects.

• It's useful to start thinking with the mind of free agent rather than a long term employee. Start advocating your services in that direction. Actively seek out contract jobs because that is something employers are more comfortable providing at the moment.

3. What Is Out Now: Job Boards as the only source of work.

What Is In Now: Websites to market your skills to a broad clientele.

- Even as recently as a decade ago, one of the largest sources of jobs was the classifieds, or other job boards. There was no B2B marketing of your skills involved. It was all blind faith that someone would see the CV you're emailing and sending someone and they would select you for an interview. In this age of web surfing, blogging and Facebook pages you are much more inclined to be invited to apply for a job rather than be clingy with the given email address of a job classified on craigslist.

- You can build websites that advertise you skill sets and experience instead of individually creating a cover letter for every different job you notice. Personal Building a personal brand and then promoting it successfully is much more likely to get you a job interview quicker than just a cruising of the daily paper for a good opportunity. . In today's economy it is better to become a magnet that attracts employers to you. You then market this personal brand proactively in order to get jobs that you may have never been offered if they had just seen your resume.

4. What Is Out Now: Being reliant on stable skill set?

What Is In Now: Constant Retooling/Reinvention?

Interesting true to life quote by www.careerfolk.com,

"Knowledge is power. Invest in yourself because you can't afford to stop learning."

A good skill set, will enable you to be prepared for most opportunities, but if you want to diversify yourself from the hundreds of people with the same skills set you have, you should constantly re-evaluate and envisage increasing the skills you have because with every new leap in technology and the constantly changing work environment, comes different requirements. Learning how to adapt to all to these changes with new skills will set you apart from the crowd. Learn everything new that pertains to your field as and when it evolves, so that you have the edge when it comes to a prospective job.

Don't pass up extraneous training on the job. Anything that helps you be better at your job is a useful tool.

5. What Is Out Now: The Company you are working for manages your career.

What Is In Now: You are the Boss and CMO of your career.

Another important traditional career perspective is that in the earlier decades your company was the manager of your career path, your advancement, and effectively your promoter. With the new information age, now you are not only the boss of your own career, it is also up to you to figure out the next move to get the career advancement that you are looking for. It is expected of you to take charge of your career and lead your –self to your own advancement. Be aware of how your career choices are affecting your chances and take a step to ensure that you are doing everything in your power to achieve the success you crave. The days of your manager making recommendations for your career advancement are in the past – it is now down to you to provide your own glowing resume by creating a great personal brand.

The new reality of the traditional paradigm stands at parallels with the recent emergence of social networks. Let's take a look at the scales for evaluating the new paradigm:

1. What is job satisfaction and what factors affect it?

Earlier we happened to talk about job satisfaction and its implications for an employee's decision to continue his or her stint in the job category they were assigned to, but what factors or characteristics of job satisfaction influence our decision to be self employed, or to be employed by a company?

According to a recent study conducted about the new career paradigm by the American Business Collaboration, there are seven scales, which affect job satisfaction and, therefore an employee's decision as whether to continue in a specific company:

Compensation: Salary/wage, benefits. This is, to some extents and purposes a no brainer. In this age of mortgages and medical bills the salary you are getting does undeniably affect your decision to stay in a company, or go for better prospects elsewhere. When you are moderately qualified and underachieving it may seem silly to risk a stable job for a better opportunity that you can only scope out from afar, but when you are driven to achieve a certain job status, or have pressing needs that make you feel the need for better salary and benefits then you will jump at the chance when a better opportunity knocks on your door.

Development: Advancement opportunity; the opportunity to learn and grow. Not everyone is at the same stage of life, i.e., not everyone has children in school, or bills that need to be paid, or have to worry about their salary. Wanting to move along on the hierarchy is just as, and in some cases, more important to some employees than to others. Education and training, career development, mentoring, coaching, and performance feedback are also looked upon as a developmental curve, which is regarded as important, especially if you are invested in your job despite the substandard pay.

Learn to evolve your job into something other than what is on the job description – it will stand you in good stead in the long run when either you are not laid off by your company – because you are too valuable or you are laid off (they had no choice) but you are superbly qualified to do other things.

Job Meaning: Meaningful work, or what is the company mission, does it keep you passionate about your job? Do you wake up every day feeling like you are doing something worthwhile? This could be anything that you subjectively think makes a difference, even in the smallest way. If you are working in a position that doesn't make you swell with the smallest hint of joy, or at least some heartfelt passion, then you will be quickly looking for a better job that keeps your interest and makes you feel better about your role.

Job Autonomy: Autonomy (control over work), having decision-making authority. Are you stuck in a job where you feel your leadership skills are be quashed, or are underutilized. Job satisfaction potential is affected negatively when employees aren't happy with being directed, or just instructed what to do anymore. Unless the instruction is helpful or beneficial – it probably isn't a good thing to hear every day of your working life. Some people are born leaders and some are alright with just following orders, but being used to your full potential is a good way to feel satisfied with your job.

Contribution: Is your job challenging enough? Is it fully utilizing your abilities? Is your opinion valued? Don't wait for opportunities to present themselves, be proactive and seek out opportunities that provide this factor. This is something of vital importance in this new age as a qualifying factor that affects the employee career choices in a big way.

Workplace Relationships: This is all about workplace collaboration, teamwork and quality of the office work culture, diversity of workforce, etc. When the workplace atmosphere is relaxed, and full of people who are at ease with you and offer working companionship in a manner of speaking, you feel like you're in the right place. This is necessary because you spend many hours of the day at a work place, and if the atmosphere is thick with unwanted tension, or full of people who are hard to get along with, it can be distracting and negatively impact your career by you choosing to leave a good job because you're unhappy. Not the smartest choice maybe, but sometimes the easiest.

Schedule Control: Flexibility, workload and work/life balance. Are you able to take a holiday without being treated like you're not taking your work seriously? Are you expected to do the work of ten people and unable to balance your work and home life. Economical downturn in most companies has cost many employees their jobs, but the work load is still present and needs to be completed by someone. The managers see themselves as having no choice, but to shift the load on the one person who can do these jobs. This might create conflict and problems for both the employer and the employee -as an employee who doesn't have better prospects might continue to do the work assigned, because they have limited options available to them. This may lead to problems, for example they may not be able to finish work on time and therefore become easily frustrated with the amount of work that their employer is expecting from them, given this circumstance, this issue may be further exacerbated as the pay may not reflect the level of work which the employee is completing.

You might think that some of these factors are a reality of the new career paradigm and some haven't really affected you - yet. There is a reason for that, something we will look into further when we continue with the next important career archetype.

2. Age – How does it affect the new job profiles?

I know what you're thinking, age? Really? Is age really an important measure in the career projection formula? Do people in their mid 20's have different career priorities to people in their 30's and mid 40's? Well, truthfully, career priorities and aspirations of different age groups are a bunch of diversified stories. A much more appropriate way to look at it would be how people in different stages of life are affected by their age pertaining to their career choices and progression.

Life changing stages and factors are different from the baby boomer generation, the new reality is that career progression and stability is given much more importance now then a few decades ago.

- Consider a twenty something graduate that has just landed a beginner job. His or her job satisfaction requirements undoubtedly differ from a thirty something employee who is settled into their job, has received a promotion or two and has invested in buying a home for future family aspirations. There are beginnings of personal fulfillment which are important for this particular age group that is out reach of typical young adulthood.

- According to March 2013 statistics the average age of marriage for women in America is 27, for men it is 29. 1990's statistics, on the other hand provided that the average age of women being married then was 23 and for men it was 26. According to this survey, women with college degrees are much more likely to have children after they are married than if they don't have college degrees.

- These factors influence the career model greatly because employees who are in different stages of life will differ in their aspirations and expectations in a job. A married father of two will expect better compensation in lieu of his family obligations and his prior experience. A college graduate who graduated from an Ivy League college would expect a prestigious job and would have different ideas in mind with regards to job fulfillment and flexibility.

- For women in their forties personal fulfillment of balancing a family life better might be their key aspiration. The new career model has changed to adapt all ages and their professional and personal requirements.

- Men in their fifties will be working towards their pension and may prefer stable job conditions to support their families, or simply just earn enough to finish paying for their houses, college fees for older children, and eventual medical bills for when they are older and susceptible to illnesses.

- Since the demographics for single men and women, and divorced spouses who are needed to pay child support has risen over the years, young mothers and single fathers are easily in need of both better jobs and pay.

Apart from age, education, geographic locations, cultural attitudes to job titles, and availability of jobs in a certain area, town, and country also plays an important role in determining job profiles in the new age, but it's easiest to make a distinction using age groups, as stages of life alter perceptions and needs in various ways.

3. **How do all these factors tie in with personal branding?**

Yes, this book has turned to career dynamics. It must seem like it's thrown itself off topic and sidetracked itself from the real topic, however, bear with me Personal branding as a concept might have existed long ago, but it has lain dormant until the introduction of social web and blogging applications.

Creating a personal brand is very much like looking for better jobs prospects, and is influenced by many of these factors that essentially make the career paradigm so relevant. Personal branding relies on all factors which contribute to discussions regarding career choices and expectations.

A job search is no longer just a job search. It's more of a self promotion process with heavy emphasis on personal branding. Career progression depends on how well connected you are and what image you project of yourself to the rest of the world through the various available platforms both offline, but increasingly online. The competition is mind boggling and the possibilities are endless in this respect. No longer can personal branding be considered a tool of those with celebrity status such as artists and millionaires. Now personal branding is like the advent of Chinese production and its subsequent victory in being a manufacturer and supplier of all products. We are in a personal branding revolution in a similar way that new technology trickles down from the early adopters to the mainstream. Now is the time to get ahead of the pack and establish a personal brand for yourself before your competition beats you to it. In the same way personal branding is a tool that everyone can use now or whenever for free. Everything you do online is construed as a potential personal branding tactic. How your popularity stays when it goes viral is how you conduct yourself online.

In summary, the new reality of the traditional career paradigm is continuously evolving. The trend of writing up job applications based just on your experience, or skills just doesn't cut it anymore. How many followers do you have on twitter and how much of your skills are noticeable through good self promotion ways is what will bring you to the forefront of a hundred and ten applications for that very same job, reliant on the same sort of experience credentials and educational statistics.

To be ahead of the pack you have to be the personal brand everyone talks about, or at least is well known enough through the interconnected web to be a company CEO's first choice. Career progression is intimately twined with personal branding objectives, or as personal branding guru Dan Schawbel says, "Why leave your Career to chance? Promote Yourself."

4. How do you find a job in the year 2014?

We have established the traditional career rules and the new ones which are dominating the online world. "What essential factors affect your job expectations and influence your career decisions, but with the recent emergence of the massive layoff culture and closing down of reputable companies, how is one meant to go about looking for a job? It's questionable because of the many hundreds of ways to approach that one job opening, or that lack of a job opening. Newspaper classifieds have a limited amount of job advertisement...compared to the internet.

Today, smart, highflying employers advertise their needs on the web, or they're head hunting technique has become a separate debate entirely as with firms such as Google, Apple or Amazon. While, the old methods of approaching potential job candidates are not considered to have faded away, they are still very much present, but in use in a more internet savvy way. Prospective employees are expected to fill complete online applications that absorb not only their general information, but also pertinent information that is relevant to a job profile posted by a company.

Earlier decades would not have bothered asking the question, or at least not all of them. Many of us now know the difficulties faced in the current job market, while looking for a job that fulfills all our needs and the employer's needs. It has become a symbiotic relationship that benefits both parties. The internet has made this possible, but you will ask though, what are those ways to approach a job market in the year 2014.

Firstly, Stop looking for a job: Yes, just what it says, stop the aimless search for a job and take the opportunity to situate yourself in the job market

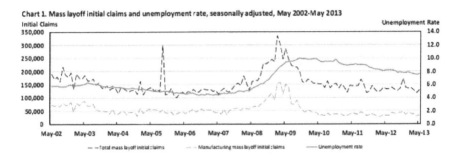

Chart 1. Mass layoff initial claims and unemployment rate, seasonally adjusted, May 2002-May 2013

properly. Looking for a job in today's work culture is not about 'the job search'. It's more about the research for it. You need to think of yourself as a scientist who is looking for answers to a medical mystery. In this case it will be to identify your skills and realize what kind of jobs they are applicable to, what companies are hiring your talent for, etc. You can't be expected to be hired for a job you don't know how to do. This saves you and the employer a lot of time and trouble and pushes you in the right direction.

If you just box yourself into one kind of job depending on the traditional career paradigm, or just misplace yourself with too many available options that you may or may not be skilled enough for, you are bound to be disappointed in your job search and will continue to blame the bad economy for your unemployment. You can beat the bad economy by being smart about how you go about acquiring your new job.

Self assessment: This is an important part of the 'not looking for a job' process. Find out all your unique characteristics that are useful to prospective employers and business partners because no one is going to look for what makes you different from all other millions of candidates that are being already screened, they are simply too short on time. You should know your strengths, weaknesses and advantages, and channel them in the right direction. This is not an easy exercise. Not all of us are good at figuring out our best professional attributes and hiring a career coach can help you recognize and articulate your strengths correctly. Alternatively, just ask some of your friends. I'm sure you know someone who is close to you who will be able to identify your strengths, weaknesses and attributes – even if you don't like some of the things that they have to say.

Self branding: Finding a job is increasingly about self branding, because self branding no longer only applies to companies and products. If you are online, you already are a brand and people are already using it to determine information about you. What you do with your brand and how you manage it to produce good results personally or professionally is up to you. The platforms to achieve all you can with your brand already exist. There are tools that can help you build a complex and sophisticated brand image. By clearly identifying your strengths, talent and passion, you are more likely to easily and effortlessly stand out from the crowd and get other people to co-operate with you.

Marketing: Marketing yourself properly can prove to be more successful if your message reaches the preferred target audience, and for this to take place along with your personal brand, you need to be able to market yourself with the appropriate aggressiveness. Marketing yourself through the internet has never been easier with scores of media applications at your disposal. The challenge lies in finding your unique selling point and competition analysis. Marketing and unique selling points go hand in hand. Learn what are the unique points about your brand that make it stand apart from others and use them in marketing yourself. Successful personal brands are well marketed and unique to all the competition. This is one of the reasons that they succeed whilst others do not.

Networking: No matter how many times you've heard about 'networking' being a great way to gain contacts and finding good opportunities, it does not get old and never gets redundant. New social network applications like Facebook, Linked In, and Twitter, etc. have made the networking process more complex in terms of integrating all these applications and using them to your advantage. Networking is a way of marketing yourself unobtrusively through others. Spend some time reading around social networking blogs and websites in order to improve both your use of this rapidly changing technology and also your understanding of it.

The importance of Personal Branding

Now we have danced around the subject of personal branding and its implications on our life as we know it. The Branding Book is all about developing a personal brand, but it is also about defining and emphasizing the factors that make it an important part of culture today. So, it is interesting to note how some of these quotes sum up our chapter title.

1. "Your brand is what people say about you when you're not in the room" - <u>Jeff Bezos</u>, Founder of Amazon

2. Branding demands commitment; commitment to continual re-invention; striking chords with people to stir their emotions; and commitment to imagination. It is easy to be cynical about such things, much harder to be successful." - <u>Sir Richard Branson</u>, CEO Virgin

3. "It's important to build a personal brand because it's the only thing you're going to have. Your reputation online, and in the new business world is pretty much the game, so you've got to be a good person. You can't hide anything, and more importantly, you've got to be out there at some level." - <u>Gary Vaynerchuk</u>, Author of '*Crush it!'*

4. "Personal Branding is a revolution in the way we manage our careers or businesses. It means identifying and communicating what makes you unique, relevant, and compelling so that you can reach your goals. Personal branding means using who you are to get what

you want from life." -William Arruda, Founder, Reach Branding Club

5. What are the benefits of personal branding?

So, if after the parade of the power quotes above if you're still wondering about the special, magical powers of personal branding and thinking why you should be a part of it, let's take into consideration how the phenomenon of personal branding affects you and in what ways does it transform for your life and career.

Develop your confidence: Personal branding has the power to give you greater confidence in yourself and in your ability to complete all the things you want to complete. Once you see all you have to offer and how your skills and experiences can contribute to your life and the lives of others your self esteem will soar, you start feeling better about yourself. Personal branding is no magic potion that will help you get your high school sweetheart, or the praise of someone coveted by you for years. It will help boost you when you need that boost the most. It all depends on how you market yourself and what you bring to the world for them to notice you. If someone notices you out there, you are doing something right.

Build your presence and credibility: There is no doubt that semi permanent internet pages will forever hold an image of you and help you get your message across, but building a presence has never been easier in today's world. Facebook, Twitter and blogs all offer various ways to make yourself known and develop a basic credibility that will leave an impression on others in a positive way if you go about it correctly.

Helps you leave your mark and have greater control and power over your career: The traditional job structure offered control of one's career mostly to the employer, now the structure has changed with the emergence social technology and you are your own boss in many ways. You have greater control on the image you build of yourself online, how you establish yourself as a brand and collate followers who will remember you from the mark you leave through your branding process.

Connects you to your target audience: Personal branding helps you connect with your target audiences, wherever they may be. Personal branding offers you the platform to communicate with the right people and build a good professional relationship with them. This is a good way to find opportunities that will help further you along the career curve ahead of others.

Diversifies you from the competition: Competition has always been there and only increases with time and the various platforms offered by viral marketing, what differentiates you from rest of the pack? Are you able to convey that to your target audience? Because this is what makes a difference, personal branding identifies your competitive edge and shows your audience what you have that others don't.

Enhances your self - awareness: When you create a personal brand that is visible to others, you will no doubt receive praise from some, but from others you will receive criticism, which might affect your personal branding decisions further down the process. This is a good thing, as you are putting yourself out there for others to judge you and if some constructive criticism comes your way you can use it to your advantage and learn from it. Personal branding not only helps you create a presence, it also tells you how others perceive you. Great values and decisions are based on the perceptions of you from your target audience.

Helps gather more wealth: Once you have a successful brand following, people will want to do more business with you because people generally like to work with an expert in their field who is also well known. Once you've achieved a reasonably good following and are pulling in the masses, your success will come in the form of wealth. If personal branding works for you, you can find a better paying job, more customers for your products etc.

More professional referrals: Once you are a successful brand that has gained some recognition, the ultimate reward of personal branding, among others is how it basically helps you in constant self promotion. You get more professional referrals from like minded individuals who view you as personal brand worth their attention.

6. **Online Tools for building a successful personal brand**

To derive the above mentioned benefits of personal branding, you need to be able to build a successful personal brand. We briefly discussed some tools earlier in the introduction of the book that help you build one. What other tools can you invest effort in that will help you differentiate yourself from others in your field.

YouTube: This is the perfect way to introduce yourself as an expert in your field. Videos talking about your brand and essentially video blogging helps build a great connection between you and the target audience. It is an interactive feature. This is not a new concept, but lately a rapidly evolving one. Last year's America's Got Talent featured wild card contestants that auditioned through YouTube and built a large following. This was the reason they got selected, because of public vote on their YouTube videos.

Many emerging artists display their talents through this tool. Music videos, comedic skits, short movies, and web series. Webinars and self promotional videos can help you tremendously in building a personal brand. Be the video everyone is passing around, or talking about.

Google Alerts: This is an application that helps you in building a personal brand by filtering internet for any mention of your name and tells you who is talking about you, in what context. It also searches the internet based on key word queries by you regarding any relevant information related to the field you are an expert in. See all the latest info, news, and updates regarding it through these alerts.

This tool can help you with self awareness and skill set improving to further qualify in your field and get better opportunities.

RSS Feed: This stands for Really Simple Syndication. If you have favorite websites that offer content that constantly fuels your personal branding fire then subscribe to it and never miss out another feed. It just makes life easier.

Tweet deck: Is a desktop application that can filter favorites, mentions and direct messages in their own separate columns. Find tweets about a particular keyword subject through searches aimed at keyword search. It is a great tool to receive up to the moment news.

Google profiles: This is a simple tool, so simple that it is sometimes overlooked. It appears at bottom of the Google search page. Filling in relevant information about yourself and linking back to all the other places on the web you reside like Facebook, Twitter and Linked In, etc. can help you put together a profile that shows others how to efficiently reach, or approach you. Don't knock it until to try it!

Google analytics: This will help you ensure who is visiting your site, when and how. Set up a free account and integrate it with your website. The best thing is that mobile and tablets form a significant part of your traffic, so make sure you take this into account when designing your site. Today there are many tools that will automatically render your site into a mobile version if it detects that customer/reader is using a mobile or tablet to access it.

Ping.fm: Being a part of most of these social networks can give you a headache when you want to update them. Fear no more, that is what ping.fm if there for. If you want to update two or more social websites, it is just a click away.

You can simultaneously update both your Facebook and twitter page, instead of opening each and having to update them separately. Ping.fm is a handy tool once you gather success in personal branding; you will find it difficult to keep up with updates everywhere you are plugged in. An alternative to this application can be Hoot shoot, which is also popularly used to manage social media participation and analyze social media traffic.

Bit.ly: Is a link shortening service that not only shortens long URL's into social media friendly links, but also tell you how many times your suggested link was clicked on. This way you can have some measurable results while working on your personal brand.

Word press: Is highly publicized blogging application that is the most recommended out of all these tools.

Blogging is the best way to bring your personal brand to the world in an accomplished way that Facebook and twitter won't do for you. A good blog page will help you get your vision across better than any of these other tools. So, invest effort and time into crafting a good image on your blog page. Create your personal branding message that you want to get across to others. Use Word press as a tool that gives others a clear and detailed view of what your personal brand is all about.

You don't even have to write the articles yourself. Look into PLR articles that you can buy on the internet, adapt them to your liking and then post them. This way, at least half of the work has been done for you. Beware however that Google and other search engines have become very good at spotting plagiarized content – don't fall into the trap of just using the same article that someone else has used – put your own unique spin on it and it will serve you better as it will compliment your personal brand.

Submitting your website to web crawlers (SEO):
Submit your website to as many search engines as possible; the more you shout about your brand, the better! Some of them are free and some are for a fee. Word press contains a built in search engine optimization tools. Make sure once you are comfortable with using Word press, you customize the tools to your websites needs.

Search engine optimization means certain key words and phrases that show up more on the internet. When you type in that phrase in a search engine you will get suggestions that lead you to various websites. Think like a web browsing customer and think what keywords they would use to search for your content, and use the keywords as seamlessly as you can in your content.

About.me: This can be a central place for all you social applications that you are a part of, to come together and create a homepage that showcases what you share with the rest of the world. Others can find out what you're all about easily from this website.

Social Mention: This tool is somewhat like Google alerts and tells you whenever you are mentioned online anywhere based on your keywords. An alternative to this tool can be Who's Talkin', that essentially tells you who is talking about you.

Namyz: Helps you quantify and rate your online presence and likeability. You can earn badges and endorsements based on your media influence which will be calculated through Namyz.

The tools are all there for your picking and representing yourself. The success of your personal brand depends to a large extent on well you manage and utilize these tools to achieve it. The route you take with these tools in building an online image of yourself will stay with you for a long time. Be both cautious and ambitious about what you representing in your personal brand and market it with credibility that will not only attract others to your online charisma, but also help you achieve your goals and aspirations.

The many tools mentioned here may make your head spin, but not to worry, you already might be using some of them for non influential purposes. Turn it around to make use of it in way that endorses your brand and builds your credibility. Be responsible for your professional engagements online.

Don't just depend on social networking applications to make all the difference. The trick is how you use them, what you put forward about yourself to others and how others perceive you. Use the rest of the tools to measure your success, or failure and learn from both experiences. This will help you achieve some semblance of control over your personal brand.

Remember,

"If opportunity doesn't knock, build a door."

– Milton Berle

7. Personal brand strategists

There are several certified personal brand strategists that boast about their powers of creating a brand identity that will facilitate you in reaching your goals. So, what is a personal brand strategist?

A personal brand strategist is someone who will manage your brand and the success that should come along with it. Online programs such as 'Reach' advertise worldwide services to clients, to help them create a name and credibility that is positively lasting because, that is the ultimate goal of any brand, whether it is personal or a professional. A brand is to be known and be in positive inference with other similarly positive brands.

Don't get me wrong, these companies are not in the business of creating false images, but rather, they take your positive attributes and elevate them to a level that generates a greater buzz than you could ever hope for without them. If you feel you are unable to effectively create a brand image that speaks to your target audience, or are stuck in work for long hours which does not allow you to work on your personal brand, then personal brand strategists are for you.

They are people who remain current in this age of changing communication and web culture. They know all about the latest tools and the best way to use them in order to enhance, or create an image online that will bring you your success.

They will work on your perceived image and help you establish a network that provides you with assurance that your personal brand is visible in positive light and by merging traditional marketing with digital media.

They will provide you with a strategy to manage your brand on your blog, social media and networks and all the same monitor your brand image for how it is looked upon by the target audience. This is the important bit, your personal brand strategy is something that can make or break you.

Personal brand strategists are experienced in creating brand images for people of differing career paths and backgrounds, and can effectively adapt your brand easily and tweak it to produce the results that you might not be able to get by trying to do it all yourself.

They have a marketing plan will adaptable features to suit every personal brand, a formula for success that will start you on your personal branding journey.

www.reachcc.com is a well known example of online personal strategist website that is full of strategists for everyone, most of these strategists are certified through training courses that are aimed at learning how to build a personal brand successfully worldwide through a successful methodology launched by personal branding guru William Arruda, he works with some of the strongest brands in the world like Disney, L'Oreal, Warner Brothers, and many more.

What particular skill sets do these personal brand strategists own?

Superior communication skills – Personal brand strategists have amazing communications skills that can persuade the interest of your target market. They should be well versed in knowing how to communicate your brand image, message, and core values through the available platforms.

Trend analyzing skills – A personal brand strategist will know about the latest trends and how they affect your target audience. This marketing tool will help a great deal in establishing a personal brand. Trend analysis is important if you want to know what's more popular Facebook or Twitter? What new social media networks add to personal brand development as good platforms for communication? What strategies have competitors applied? All these things will keep a personal brand strategist busy whilst they figure out where you will fit in.

Personal brand designing skill – Gleaning the best information and designing an authentic brand from it should be a practiced skill of a personal brand strategist. They should be able to recognize your strengths and use those as the core values of your personal brand and complete the elements of personal branding, which we already spoke about in the beginning of this book.

Personal brand promotion skills – The most important skill a personal brand strategist has will be to promote a personal brand beyond a reasonable doubt and bring it success in the form of potent promotion. Everywhere. Everywhere, necessary at least, enough to get captivate an audience. Blog posts planning, website color scheme advice, advice on slogans and by lines etc. These are all things a brand strategist should know how to manage effectively. If they don't – find a new one.

Since, online personal branding is a more recent concept you can say, personal brand consultants and strategist are swiftly emerging out of the wood work. In earlier, less competitive times only large companies hired people to create their brands, whilst smaller firms and celebrities used brand managers, marketing managers, or brand strategists But now, as personal branding has taken the internet by storm, personal brand strategists are also conquering this new territory on the web. After all, demand begets supply.

8. **What are the personal risks of being attached to a brand concept that failed?**

Kaplan Mobray says in his book *'10Ks of Personal Branding'*,

"Sometimes we don't reach objectives because we took a risk. When we take a risk we extend ourselves outside the zone of what we define as 'achievable'."

Failure to achieve your goals and failing a brand concept can prove be a difficult experience, but it's not unrecoverable, or something you should hide in terror from. Failure is not a recommended plan of action, and it can be said that more times that when you fail it's usually because you didn't have a plan of action, or your plan of action was the wrong plan.

Think of it as a risk that didn't pay off – but it could have done.

There are a few disadvantages that may seem unforeseeably debilitating if you are new to this, but failure can have many advantages that you weren't previously aware of.

- You can measure where the biggest areas of your success lie. What ways was the brand successful and what you did right could be used to recreate and rebrand the next concept.
- The best thing about failure is that along with the right you also get to find out everything you did wrong. This will help you with the next brand concept development.
- You will be able to see what activities were not the best use of your time last time you brand failed and

how to re-do some of the things you did wrong the last time. It's inevitable, no matter how much all of might want to

- Maybe you need to learn more about the topics you are representing, after all new information and technology is discovered every day. Keep an update of what you know about your brand concept and how to enhance it.

- Take to take responsibility for your actions and don't blame other people for it. This will prove to be harder, as it is human nature for most of us to look for blame elsewhere when we fail, but let this failure humble you and make you susceptible to learning from your mistakes to find the way forward.

Lastly, make failures a part of your personal branding. This will in effect humanize you and your brand and it gives you a good back story for future success. All in all failure does not have completely negative impact on your image. So, don't let failure define the trajectory of your career. Just roll with the punches and come out strong.

'I've failed over and over and over again in my life, and that is why I succeed.' - Michael Jordan.

Chapter 4 - Communicating your brand and goals online through Facebook, Twitter, Linked and SEO blogs.

Many people think communication can only be verbal and that a picture says a lot about you, but what does that picture say about you when communicate without saying anything at all? Personal branding can be a powerful tool online, if communicated effectively. We discussed previously that myriads of applications can make that happen, but how do you go about using them? What are the basic etiquettes of using Facebook to communicate your brand to the world?

You could just join Facebook and a few other social media networks. Make a profile in everyone of them and hope for a turnover of a few hundred interested people in your personal brand, but this will be wishful (and foolishly optimistic) thinking. Virtually everyone these days owns a Facebook account, but every Facebook account does not equal an effective personal brand. A personal brand is about garnering interest of others, having doors opened to you that were previously not there, and achieving personal goals that you are aiming to achieve by joining all of these social networks.

It might seem silly to obsess over these details, but they can make all the difference to your brand image. Using social media to create followers and maximize your likes might come to you naturally, or it may not, but there are certain rules when it comes to updating and maintaining appropriate standards of professionalism on your social media pages, which if you build upon with some seasoned guidance, you will find yourself not having to work too hard on promoting your personal brand.

The way you communicate your message whether verbally or non-verbally says a lot about your image. More important than this, is what are you communicating about yourself to others unintentionally because you cannot control what you do not recognize.

1. Researching your competitors

This is an essential step in letting the rest of the world get a first look at your personal brand and what it stands for, but before we get into the basics of what message communicating should entail, let's go ahead and look at what is the first and most important part of this process: Research.

I mentioned this earlier when discussing how research is important to help you get a good job, but here, our main focus is how personal branding as a whole will contribute to that effect and find you that professional success that you are coveting. Researching your competitors in the market is not the equivalent of sneaking a look someone else's test paper. It's more of learning to find an advantage through self assessment. Researching your competitors who are, after all, in direct competition with you in the same field will help you asses where you stand, what you lack, and what you are better at. These are all valid questions that should help you massively while constructing your message. If you don't do it – they will and who do you think will lose out then?

Apply a SWOT analysis to yourself as a complete self assessment to see where you stand in terms of your Strengths as a brand, your Weaknesses, where do Opportunities lie for you, and lastly what are the Threats to your brand identity development? This is an important step in developing your message. You want it to be natural and authentic, not something you just put together hastily when you encountered some recent competition. Failure to plan is as bad as planning to fail.

2. **Developing your Message**

This is the first, most important, part of the process that you must invest time and effort in. What is your message? We have already discussed how to get it across to a captive audience. You just need to know what your own message and personal brand is all about - developing a message for your personal brand is all about:

- Effectiveness in the way it is understood by others. If your message is not clear and others are not connecting with your vision, you need to change the way you are putting your message across. Know your audience and their preferences when it comes to messages. Again, take the time to research your target audience and your past mistakes if any (be honest!).

- Is it memorable and unique to others? Does your message stand out at all, or is it much the same as the rest of your competitors? You need to be unique in a sea of similar talent. Your message should be the one that other people can easily remember.

- The persuasiveness of your brand identity and its message. How persuasive are you in bringing people closer to your brand and allowing them to take an interest in you. The degree of persuasion depends on the way you market your message and, whether your message is likeable enough.

So while building your message, make sure that you know what your values are and what you are trying to bring across to the rest of the world because unless you know what your own message is all about it cannot be effective in terms of the delivery. Seek out your message and your goals for the message. Ask yourself these questions:

- How many people do you want your message to reach? Segregate your target audience and make sure they are getting your message appropriately. Check back on responses and likes from others, and be sure to appreciate comments interested readers give you. Show them some virtual courtesy and gratitude. Let them know that you are aware of their interest and build rapport with them. Even negative or crucial comments can present this opportunity to you. There is nothing bad about feedback – even if it is negative.

- How many people have already responded to your previous personal branding message? What part of the target audience successfully understood the message you were trying to get across, and what were the positive interactions you had with them? Knowing this is really important if you want to maximize your potential of a better response in the future.

- What were the failing points of that last message? We talked about the failure of a personal brand before and the importance of knowing what activities subsequently hinted towards the failure of a personal brand. When you are building a personal brand, your learning curve never finishes. There are always new things you can learn about the way you conduct your brand image that you were previously unaware of. For example, we talked about failure earlier; it is not the end of the world. It is just furthering you along the learning curve. So, learn to analyze problems with your brand, and take steps to improve your mistakes.

The more mistakes you make, the more you are attempting to succeed.

Let's talk about some famous personal brands:

Steve Jobs is someone who is known for his 'be unique', 'be different' personal brand position. The recent movie 'Jobs' depicts many different strategies he employed to create a personal brand that would be memorable. He is someone who literally lived his brand, the way he wanted to and not the way others wanted him to make the brand. This is proof that unique brand positioning plays an important role in the way your brand develops and expands.

Someone like Oprah Winfrey's, whose brand philosophy is all about empowering other people through her brand's authentic influence, uplifting stories, and heartwarming advice. She is true a rags to riches story. Her personal brand translates into acceptance of oneself. It all about who you are, where you came from, and understanding where you want to be in the future, She has, over the years related to her audience through empathy, and is crystal clear about her brand's purpose.

Both these individuals were all about passion and had a clear purpose in their mind. This is something that is of utmost importance if you are looking to create a strong brand image that others respond to. If you have something unique to offer to the world that you are sure will gather everyone's interest and support, you should work to first find your passion and define a clear purpose for your personal brand. Others will follow you, with time.

When you look at other success stories such as, Seth Godin, Guy Kawasaki, Richard Branson, Sara Blakely, and Brit Morin, etc. each of them carry similar traits like Steve Jobs and Oprah Winfrey – passion and purpose.

They are well aware of what they have to offer and what they want to do with it. Their passion and purpose has dredged a clear path forward for them and made them successful at what they do. Loving what you do is also important if your search for passion finds a roadblock. Think about what you love doing and translate that into your brand identity.

The Foundation Step - Your Passion.

Without a burning passion you would do hard to find a unique personal brand. Find you passion, go a self discovery mission. Learn about yourself and what you want others to know about you.

Dig down deep to understand:

If you dig deep enough inside yourself you will discover what you are passionate about. There are some major pivot points in life that can shape a personal brand.

- Think of what you enjoy doing most.

- Think of your inspirations and how they tie into your aspirations.

- Think of what excites you most, what stories inspire you.

- Think of stories you've read that have brought you closer to your passion, or brought a kink in your way of thinking.

- Try travelling and expanding your circle of friends.

- Try to come out of your comfort zone attend events that are outside your area of expertise.

- If you've had some negative experiences you might be able to channel those negative emotions into a positive brand image. So, use these negative memories of places, people in your life, etc. to discover your passion.

This might seem like an unnecessary process that is like some filler exercises that you would like to avoid, but it's actually helpful to the brand image development if you're serious about creating a noticeable brand that helps you achieve goals. List out all your passions and goals in life, persistence helps with those blocks you may experience during the process.

"Change itself has changed. Management consultants have declared that change used to be a bridge to a new road, BUT NOW IT IS THE ROAD.

Unfortunately, that notion won't fly with most organizations accustomed to making a risk-averse move only after receiving a signal that a shift was already underway." - Mark Affleck, CEO of YellowChair Strategy, will give you great insights into the Passion and Purpose equation.

The bottom line is to find your unique selling preposition and use that to further your brand development.

The Foundation Step - Your Purpose

If you've made it this far, it means you already have your passion in mind and know that having a purpose gives you and your personal brand a meaning and direction, without these two you have no destination.

'If you don't know where you are going, any road will get you there.' - Lewis Carroll

Imagine investing your time, or money in someone who you're unable to understand. If their message is unclear you won't want to invest in someone who does not know what direction they want their personal brand to have.

Simplifying Your Purpose

'Our prime purpose in this life is to help others. And if you can't help them, at least don't hurt them.' - Dalai Lama

'The purpose of our lives is to be happy.' - Dalai Lama

Inspiring, someone is a fulfilling characteristic of a personal brand, but how you inspire someone depends on what platform you choose to deliver your message and the skills you accumulate along the way. It can be complicated when you are trying to find the purpose of your life, but we can try to simplify the process.

Start with trying to aligning both purpose and passion together with:

- What your skill sets are,

- And realizing what you have to offer others and how this can improve the quality of someone else's life.

  Let's try looking at this from another perspective, try to extract keywords from your resume and answer the following two questions:

- What are your primary skill sets?

- Do you know how can you help people with your primary skill sets?

  This may seem like an over simplistic point of view about building a foundation to find your passion, but a simplified way works better and get's your foot in the door.

  As Steve Jobs once said:

"You can't connect the dots looking forward; you can only connect them looking backwards. So you have to trust that the dots will somehow connect in your future. ... This approach has never let me down, and it has made all the difference in my life."

For most of us, learning your purpose can be an ongoing effort and it may involve your thought process evolving through it, just try to keep asking yourself:

- What am I unique at?

- What makes me feel like I'm valued?

- And am I betraying myself?

Asking yourself these three questions will bring you closer to realizing your dream of the purpose of your life. Source - http://www.garyhyman.com/5-easy-steps-to-build-an-effective-social-media-content-strategy/

3. Focusing on your benefits and USP as a brand

Focusing on your benefits as a personal brand:

"If you don't know what you bring to the table, you don't get a seat there." - Dan Shawabel

As a personal brand, you should be promotional about the strengths of your brand, its unique selling points and how it critically benefits others, instead of being more concerned with communicating your brands features.

Features and benefits are completely different from each other in many ways. One of the ways it's different is that features are generally available and noticeable to anyone, but benefits can be hard to understand unless you communicate those through the appropriately available channels at your disposal. Once you get others to notice your unique features as a brand you will take a huge step towards achieving your goals.

4. Key message delivery

Effective message delivery is not all about being robotic in your approach, it's more about delivering the key points of your message properly and repeatedly in a way that attracts others to you. As long as your key message is short, clear, and it incorporates all those important points that makes your brand sought after you will have a good response.

5. Social media communication

"Proficiency in social media is a differentiator now, but will soon be a qualifier." - Dan Shawabel

Facebook? Twitter? There are so many Social networks to choose from.

We all know the various ways we can socially connect with the world through Facebook and all casual networking applications that allow us to leave behind a certain amount of obscurity, but how much do we know about Facebook as a personal branding tool?

Facebook can be a powerful tool which showcases what your brand is really all about, but it's not the only one as we saw in earlier chapters. There several other social media applications that millions are currently a part of and are enjoying the exposure these applications give them on a personal branding level. All have differing features of varying positives, but is joining all of them crucial? Or can two or three suffice in the beginning? We will look into that a little later. For now let's see some of the social media etiquettes that will help you break ice with these social applications.

Evaluate your Social Media page (Facebook / Twitter / Linked In)

Evaluation of your profile and page means literally, what does your Facebook page say about you? Your personal Facebook page will be viewed by many people, such as dates, teachers, potential employers, and business partners, etc. So, take a good long at what your page says about you as a personal brand because all of us, who own these semi permanent public records, are in reality a personal brand already. We are putting ourselves out there for others to judge us. If you want your personal brand image to soar positively, make sure you know what your page is reflecting about you.

Does your Facebook page reflect your personal life too much? Personal brand development sometimes gets a leg up when the person behind a personal brand seems human and relatable, but a balance in necessary in this matter because if you have personal matters, or personal beliefs embellishing on, which may negatively impact on your image, then you need to keep your personal profile separate and private.

Are you speaking to your target audience?

This again is another key factor which can make a substantial difference in personal brand development and its success. If you're not communicating your personal brand to the right audience you will not get the expected results. If your audience is not being reached, you will find your message not making the impact you hoped for. Those prospective employers will not call you up for an interview because they are not the ones the message is directed towards.

Target market and trend analysis are important factors that facilitate a brand development, or keep you from diverting energy in the wrong direction. If you're a fashion designer than continuously posting in a make-up/cosmetics group will do nothing to help you find a target market that will buy for you, you need to target your message at fashion models, photographers, and fashion designing groups.

Assess your brand values

What do you want your personal brand to say about you on your Facebook page? Make sure you know your core values and whether you have they are actively displayed on your Facebook page in terms of your actions and words. We talked about brand values in the earlier chapters and how they are the cornerstones of an authentic brand.

Are your brand values reflected on your page, if so are they getting your core values across to your visitors? What do others think of these values? Measure your success in personal branding according to relevant response from your target audience. Your likes on your Facebook page and the amount of activity on your page should easily tell you whether your brand values have been received as you intended by others.

Set your privacy settings

Privacy settings on Facebook are helpful for many things. Such as:

- Keeping unwanted attention at bay.
- Making sure only the selected audience view and comment on your content. Competitors can view a limited profile of you.
- You can block spammers who fill you page with unwanted adverts and tags that clutter your page with too much information that the target audience isn't interested in.

- Controlling who sees your information; you can make some parts of your profile public and some parts of it private for new users.

Don't give everyone access to your page, filter your contacts and make sure you have reputable and helpful contacts that will further your personal brand in positive manner instead of having a negative effect on your brand. The privacy settings change in Facebook regularly so keep up with Facebook's privacy topics and make sure all your bases are covered.

Fill out your profile completely

If you're Facebook strategy is to create connections online through contacts be sure to fill in education and work section of your profile extensively, this can help you find a better job, get more opportunities to promote your personal brand, or just form good connections that can positively reinforce your brand image and provide you a social proof of your expertise in your niche.

Facebook is a great platform to connect with influential individuals who can both promote you and provide you with good contacts. You can fill in what school you went to, where you worked and this can lend authenticity to your page, which is something people appreciate. Half the time people lie about their profiles in order to make themselves seem more attractive to other people. The more you fill your profile with authentic answers the more recognition you will receive in the long run.

Import contacts and grow your network

Facebook offers a great feature to import your contacts whether they may be from your email account and instant messengers. You can add friends from your blog through Facebook connect and it will not only import your friends, but this gives you a good option to promote your content through whatever social interactions you have online on your blog.

Update your status

Keep people informed about updated content on your website through your Facebook statuses. Have any upcoming events? Just give a shout out to your audience through your status, so that they know about it and your content is reviewed by others. Use this feature to promote your content regularly and inform others of other upcoming specially featured content. Not updating statuses will just make your profile seem not that much exciting and will not interest your target audience. I would aim to update your social media statuses around three times a day, coinciding with just after meal times, say 10:00, 15:00 and 20;00. Don't be afraid to repeat information – it takes, on average, seven repeat posts before someone actions a social media request.

Reminding readers of your new content, or bringing attention to previous content that may have become of interest again due to some trend fluctuation is a good way to promote your content, website, and personal brand. Updating your status regularly will give the air of someone who is involved and interactive. Those are two crucial things you will need to be if you want your content to be liked and followed more than your competitors.

Start a group, or a page

Facebook groups have fewer features in them than 'actual' facebook pages, but you can use videos, links etc to promote your personal brand and interact with others on your group page. It's a good thing to use these efficiently and create a personal connection with your chosen target audience.Use these features to attract more people towards your core message through taking maximum advantage of features provided by Facebook.

Your Facebook page will allow your brand to 'go viral' and is not only for high profile people like celebrities, high ranking officials and products, or well known companies. You can also use it for personal brand development. So, joining a group, or creating one will make you different from other brands. Especially, if you're personal brand is gaining success through your group – which it should!

Join or start an event in your area

One of the best aspects of Facebook is that you can get involved in your community by joining or starting an event in your category. When you open up your event to others, you can find others who share your interests and can help you by supporting your career. You can catalogue events on your Facebook page, using the 'create an event' feature on Facebook.

If you're looking to start a weekly or monthly event and want to include it on a calendar, it's good strategy to put it on your page. By doing this, you're able to position yourself as an expert in your field, and this is good for your personal branding image.

Tips for your Twitter profile

To new users, twitter can certainly appear to be a form of organized chaos. How can you go about starting a successful personal brand on Twitter when there are literally thousands of tweets that are being sent each minute, every day, or this very second? It's completely overwhelming to a new person to think about the various twitter jargon, hash tags, re-tweet features, etc that are available along with much useless information that you will have to learn to overpower before you can begin.

Building a strong personal brand is not something easy and it likely to some time before you have a successful following on Twitter But there are several tips to using Twitter which may come in handy before you start sifting through Twitter's overwhelming world and get further towards a worthy personal brand.

The key to establish your personal brand on Twitter and to build a relevant audience is to decide what you're all about.

- What is your interest in Twitter? Personal or professional? What are you looking to express about yourself and your image on twitter?

- Which interests do you have and would like to be able to represent on Twitter, or be a part of?

- In what field are you looking to actually establish yourself?

- Again, what is your passion, and what are your brand values?

  Once you know the answer to all these questions, you are ready to focus on managing your twitter account. So, what does managing a twitter account really entail?

  Profile: Your profile should be a culmination of the four questions mentioned above. Your profile should be the very embodiment of the answers to all those questions about your profile on Twitter. This establishes the crucial aspects of a personal branding like audience attention to you, or why would someone, anyone, follow you on Twitter? Don't be hasty, but don't be shy either. Fill your profile completely just like your Facebook page and link them both by regular usage of similar brand values and voice on both pages, so that others recognize and know you from both profiles.

Hashtags: This is a phenomenon that rivals a social media network. People use hashtags on twitter to get find tweets with similar topics. Take for example the recent typhoon in Philippine's; some of the tweets probably had #Haiyan in them. It's just searching for tweets with common topics. Elizabeth Kricfalusi who writes for Tech for Luddites on www.techforluddites.com talks extensively about hashtags and their function on Twitter.

URL's – Provide URL's to your content in your tweets. Whenever you write new content, send out a tweet to let everyone. Even if they are in you twitter profile, they might not know about your content unless you advertise it regularly.

Twitter followers – Follow all the right people, instead of just following celebrities. Unless, they are a contributing factor to your personal brand in some way, and need to be referenced.

Re-tweeting – Re-tweeting is about repeating another users tweet, or updates whenever they update. Re-tweeting someone's content is a good way to increase your twitter following and get people engaged in your personal brand as well as content.

Profile Upgrade- When you create a website, you make sure the aesthetics are pleasing and in some small way contribute to the popularity of your website. People are attracted to certain colors and themes. So, design your twitter page and make it attractive enough to warrant a following.

Social media E's (Educate, Entertain, and Engage) – The www.tengoldenrules.com teaches us social media's three E's. According to its social media theory people are more likely to follow you on twitter and stay interested if your page has interesting, educational links and valuable information. Engaging a reader and interacting with them and replying to their comments and questions is another social media 'E' that is of utmost importance, and gives you a chance to build a rapid rapport with your audience. The last 'E' is about entertaining your readers. This is a crucial aspect of what gives your profile personality. Sharing funny YouTube videos, good music, etc. gives audience a chance to see you as more than just an avatar on a computer screen, you're a real person after all. Let your personality shine through these social media E's.

Sources – Providing sources for your material, gives your profile and personal brand more credibility. Also, if you're using someone's material, it's a good idea to credit them, instead of infringing upon someone's copyright. This is vitally important with articles and other 'published' content – don't get caught out!

Who to follow on Twitter – this is much debatable and frequently asked question, as a personal brand that is trying to find success, who should you follow?

Celebrities? High profile business entrepreneurs? Or just people who have a large following?

- Follow people who come within your niche, or are interested in your category.
- Follow ordinary people who just share your interests.
- Follow high profile entrepreneurs, if only they can be of mutual befits to you and are relevant to your personal brand image.
- Don't follow celebrities because it won't make you seem credible, or serious.
- Don't decide on not following someone based on how many twitter followers they have. Check their credentials and figure out whether their network of followers, etc. can help you promote you and your content.

Search Twitter Directories:

- **Twellow:** This is a twitter directory which you can search for a topic you are interested in and get a list of all accounts which are tagged to that topic.

- **Twtrland:** This is also a directory of twitter accounts that show statistics of how much someone with a twitter account tweets, etc. This can be useful in deciding whether to start following them on Twitter.

- **ManageFlitter:** Gives varying values which allow you to decide whether to follow, or unfollow someone. You can clear up any clutter on your account this way.

6. What is the power of blogging?

'Blogging efficiency should play a key role in your personal branding success strategy' – Roger Parker

From the year 2001, has been treated as a personal diary that would be online. This personal diary has evolved to a whole business page that communicates and embodies your brand values and mission statement. An efficient brand strategy is to have a page that delivers all the best attributes of your brand online to the target audience. You can use your blog as an online diary, or you can host content on it which others are interested in. Either ways blogging is a great way to achieve success as a personal brand. The brand development on a blog is more three dimensional than something you expect from social media applications like Facebook or Twitter. Blogging gives your personal brand a more direct and human touch, it makes you seem more real and has the potential attract many readers if you post good and valuable content.

Before posting any content, research what your readers are interested in, what are the hot topics of the moment that you are dying to write about and wanting to express views, which others would like to hear? Of course before getting strategically involved in your brand development on your web page, you will need to establish a web page first and there are several things that beginners are always grasping at the straws about and are unable to get their website up and running because setting up a blog page, or website can seem really complicated, especially if you have never attempted it before.

7. Blogging tips to help get you started:

If you are using Word press, an incidentally great blogging application that has all manners of features which will propel your personal branding journey and it will give your brand much needed depth that other social networking applications can't always provide. So, how do you go about creating an efficient blogging website?

"Once you have an efficient blogging system you'll find it relatively easy to take the next steps, like compiling your blog posts into longer publications, like books, e-books, and white papers." – Dan Shawabel

Word Press Setup

Do your homework first and read about others' mistakes: This is a good way of making sure that you are not committing those first time errors, which so easily could have been avoided. Read web reviews of others blogs and go to blog forums where newbie mistakes are discussed openly. You are more likely to gain insight from them than get confused.

Choosing a reliable web host: Web hosting plays a major part in how your website content is delivered your audience - choose wisely. So, choosing the right one is of paramount importance. Your audience will want to be able to access every website feature you have whether it's day or night, and if you have a good web host they can manage all this without too much concern.

So, how do websites work? Well, your websites files, which will be a bunch of html files, CSS files, and images which are held on a remote computer server, this is referred to as a web host. You will be paying a separate fee for this service every month. So, you can see why it's important to have a reliable web host. Design costs and domain name costs are separate from this. This remote computer that is connected to the internet will have your websites files hosted on it.

The first thing would be to choose a domain name – meaning a website address like www.sonyacupcakes.com. For an address you'll have to use a domain name registrar like Namecheap.

What is down time? - Down time on your website refers to the time your website may not be online due to a server problem. Every minute our website is down and not working a potential customer, client, or prospective client may not be able to access your website. Significant traffic needs a good web server that can handle the amount of traffic on your website and not cause an overload. This is one of the most common mistakes of new website builders while choosing a server always make sure you keep in mind the website traffic you experience, not that bandwidth and disk space isn't important. It all depends on the size of the traffic your site experiences unless you are already popular you will use hardly 10% of your bandwidth, and it can usually be increased at a later date when your popularity improves.

Use search engines and customers reviews to tell you about all the best web hosts available so that you make an informed decision. Look for a company that offers reasonable specifications and does not oversell itself.

Your web host should also give you separate email accounts that link's your site together because you are more likely to use separate email accounts for your personal needs, professional needs, and business need's .

Cloud hosting or dedicated server hosting - what's the difference?

A dedicated server hosting will dedicate an online server service to you in which you have to also help maintain the hardware. If the traffic to your website it too much for it to handle, your drive might fail, causing hours long downtime. Cloud hosting on the other hand handles the hardware for you and supports the whole platform. It's a group of servers that powers each side. If one fails, it is automatically removed and taken care of on your behalf. This means no down time as the server automatically scales and makes room for more traffic. Most people opt for cloud servers.

Live service customer?

It is essential to have live customer service in the case of any and all website problems that you may face in the foreseeable future 7 days a week, 24 hours a day. For this purpose you may do better by opting for a full service web design company.

Before signing up make sure you check the customer care service by sending them some emails to the sale support. See how quickly they respond, how friendly they are and their technical knowledge just to get a feel of what other services by the company might be like if you are to sign on with them.

Choosing a good domain name: A good domain name will attract users to at least visit your website. Try coming up with a name that is relevant to the content on your website or that is relevant to the personal branding image that you are trying to develop. Something like that will only work when you're target audience agrees with you virtually. A good domain name will be memorable, short, easily pronounceable, and relevant.

Brainstorm Five Top Keywords: What is your personal brand all about, what is your blog about? Think about the kind of target audience you want your blog reading and come up with keywords what will define those.

Make the Domain Unique: This is important. If your domain name is similar to other irrelevant sites with content that has nothing to do with what you are promoting you will confuse your target audience and they will visit these other websites instead of yours. So, make sure your domain name differs from others.

Only Choose Dot-Com Available Domains: If you're serious about creating a personal brand and a successful website that runs for a long period of time you need to own a .com website because it is more recognizable and most people just assume that .com is all that's out there. So, don't lose traffic to others.

Make it Easy to Type: Your domain should be unique to the extent that others remember it and are able to type it in to the web browser. Something that has too many numbers or other unintelligible characters may put users off visiting your website. Even if they manage to type in the domain name and then save it to their favorites, you still may have lost those crucial few people who could make all the difference.

Make it Easy to Remember: A domain name should be something everyone can pick up on easily and remember. You don't want a great website that others can remember or tell others about easily.

Keep the Name as Short as Possible: Long names with long strings of numbers and characters are not recommended as domain names because the shorter and snappier you domain name is the more memorable and easy to remember it will be.

Create and Fulfill Expectations: You domain name should reflect your content, it's as simple as that. People instantly visualize what they might find at your website based on your domain name.

Avoid Copyright Infringement: Before you buy a domain name be sure to check it's unique and does not infringe upon copyright.

Set Yourself Apart with a Brand: Just what the title says, set yourself apart from the millions of websites out there with a unique domain name that does not only embody what the content is all about, but also has a kick to it and is compelling enough for someone to take notice.

Don't Follow the Latest Trends: As tempting as they may seem, website names that rely on odd misspellings (like many Web 2.0 style sites), multiple hyphens (like the SEO-optimized domains of the early

2000's), or uninspiring short adjectives (like "top...x," "best...x," "hot...x") aren't always the best choice. Don't go with it just because others are doing it.

Register and keep your domain name with a registrar: It seems that having your domain name registered with your hosting company might be actually a bad idea. It is very likely, over the years that you may need to or might want to change your web host. It could be due to numerous reasons you might find a more interesting plan somewhere else, or simply might need to switch to a dedicated server due to increasing traffic on your website. If your hosting company is also managing your domain name they might give you a headache before performing the required changes on the name servers (i.e. making the domain point to the new host).

www.dailyblogtips.com recommends this solution - "The solution for this problem is to keep all your domains names registered with a reliable registrar (GoDaddy and eNom are known as good ones) while having a separated company to take care of the web hosting. Apart from avoiding trouble with name server changes and domain transfers this method will also be more efficient to manage your portfolio of domain names."

Always install Word Press in the root directory: If you are not sure what this means, get someone to install word press for you on a website such as fiverr.com.

Update your ping list: (Word Press users can modify their ping list on the Control Panel, and going to Options, then Writing).Ping list automatically informs your blog directories when you make updates to your blog.

Themes & Design- How are a theme and design important to a blog? They are just as important as your key message that you are trying to deliver from this platform. If your Word Press page does not visually deliver this message, you will lose some reader base. You website should reflect the personal brand you are trying hard to establish. It does not have to be high tech, but just appealing enough to intrigue some viewers on impact.

Choose a professional theme: choosing themes that are professional looking add to your personal brand a certain charm, which attracts others. If you theme is too plain, boring or too comical you won't necessarily get the right kind of audience. Always think of the kind of target audience you have and what they would appreciate in your theme.

Social media widgets: You make have seen, these days most websites support these widgets. They are buttons for social media icons and can be of immense help while marketing and promoting your website. Having these icons on your website make it easier for a user to share your post, or blog etc with others. It's like buyers impulse when users see something they like and want to share with others; they can easily click on the share, or follow button on your website. This will give you and your content a lot more exposure. You can copy past HTML codes to your site that will embed the icon/button on your site.

http://blog.hubspot.com/blog/tabid/6307/bid/2954 4/The-Ultimate-Cheat-Sheet-for-Creating-Social-Media-Buttons.aspx gives you all the details on how to get these widgets and have them on your website. They also have a lengthy discussion on what is better a twitter share button or a twitter follow button.

8. **Blog posts planning - What can you do to maximize personal branding success through your blog?**

1. Plan your blog posts offline

You should start to plan your blog posts during your downtime. The important elements that should appear in a blog post are: the title, the main ideas, and the tips at the bottom.

For this you will only needed one planning sheet; other times. However, it takes three or four tries, on different pieces of paper, to get it right. The title of every blog post is subject to many changes before you submit your final post.

2. Just write the first draft as quickly as possible

The way to succeed with blog posts is to write your first post fast without thinking too much about it, or judging yourself too much. This is a good way to prevent procrastination. When you simply write down your thoughts you might get really good, innovative ideas.

It's a good idea to save your post by copy pasting it on a word document to Writing your posts in Word Press will help you because watch the post take shape, preview what you have written from the reader's perspective, with subheads and lists. (But as you are writing it may be a good idea to copy past your posts to a word document file, to stave off the frustration of losing content.)

Also while writing your draft make sure you constantly save the draft because a great idea might come to you which you may not be able to recreate if you lose the data.

3. Put the blog post away, then edit

Instead of running the risk of being panicky about post deadlines, it's a good idea to write your draft and put it aside for a while and then return to it after maybe half an hour or a few hours or so for editing purposes.

This is meant to be 'a two day' approach so that you aren't backlogged and aren't worried about impending deadlines. Don't work in a panic driven marathon session, just pace your writing and try to work in small working sessions so that your blog post is well written and edited before final posting.

4. Print and edit one last time

Give your post a good, thorough edit by printing it on as paper. When you print your post on a page, it makes it much easier to locate errors, awkward, too long sentences, etc all are more apparent on a printed sheet than the computer screen.

This also creates an archive of your best blog posts, which you put in a three holes punched binder that can be a good way to save good

9. Getting more blog audience

Join blogging communities

Blogging communities is a way to increase your blog audience, and open you up to scores of bloggers who are writing content in your niche, you can trade, learn, and promote each other's content through these communities.

Triberr: This is a great community which hosts tribes that correspond to your contents niche. Get posting and join a tribe, find people who are hungry to read your content. This community gives you a platform to amplify your message to a much larger audience.

Social buzz club: This is similar to Triberr and allows you to post content in your desired category, or niche and then promotes it to users and followers who are looking for content in this niche.

Biz blogging buzz: According to http://www.steamfeed.com/25-smart-ways-promote-latest-blog-post/ it says that B3 Is to "connect, mastermind, make friends, learn from others, help others, provide value, showcase your talents, get your message out and have your voice heard, gain traffic to your website, monetize your passion and ultimately BE YOURSELF in business."

Viral Content buzz: This is a community of like minded bloggers who share other content and get's points for it and then add their own content to it. These website/communities are a great way to boost your web content popularity and gain a larger audience from the ones you started with.

Bookmark (Manual): This way you can open up your content to many potential readers for content that is within your niche specifically. Reddit, Scoop, StumbleUpon, Digg, and Delicious are the several known bookmarking websites that easily categorize your content into the right category and shares it with others who are looking for it. There are automated versions of bookmarking if you don't have the time to post your content to each site individually like SocialMarker, SocialADR, and Onlywire. Also always make sure that you have plug-ins available on your website, or blog that allows other people to bookmark your website such as Sociable, Shareaholic, and Nextscripts.

Comment on other blogs: Comments on blogs within your category, or niche. This is good way to get others to notice your content, acquire influencers and form strategic partnerships that will be mutually beneficial.

Share on Facebook / Linked In / Twitter / YouTube / Instagram: Share the link to your post on your social media applications that you are a part of already. Whenever you are posting a new article your social media followers can get whiff and follow, this will increase your audience and get you more attention. This will give you a consistent and cohesive personal branding marketing strategy that actually works!

There many other small things you can do to attract a customer/reader/following base that helps lift your personal brand off the ground and makes you well known, but these are the important concepts that should be your immediate focus when you start your own blog.

Pay Wall: Every brand needs a 'pay-wall', this is somewhere where you decide to stop giving away free information and offer a means of payment if customers want more information. For example, New Scientist does this by giving you the introduction of the article. It is generally suggested that you put a lot of material before the pay-wall as, the more you put before it, the higher your conversion rate through the pay-wall will be. There are pay walls that you can 'establish' after you are certain that you are getting traffic on your website. Don't give away everything for free...all the time.

To summarize, using money to motivate people can be a double-edged sword. For tasks that require cognitive ability, low to moderate performance-based incentives can help. But when the incentive level is very high, it can command too much attention and thereby distract the person's mind with thoughts about the reward. This can create stress and ultimately reduce the level of performance."

— Dan Ariely, The Upside of Irrationality: The Unexpected Benefits of Defying Logic at Work and at Home

Are you looking for clients/customers for your brand? Do you provide a service? You need to perform the equivalent of a pay-wall that those information services provide. Provide the first 50 customers with a FREE service but make sure that you get testimonials from them. They will probably be friends and family so will be unlikely to pay you anyway. Chances are, anyone who gets something for FREE will think that it is great and therefore give you a great review (and possibly recommend you to others). But make sure they know the VALUE of your service by quoting it or they may think they are getting a devaluation of your true service. And if your intention still lies in giving away free content and promotion through social media for the foreseeable future, you can maybe get a free website to host your content, instead of paying for it. There are a host of FREE hosting companies on the internet today. From Moonfruit.com to Webs.com they all provide you with a free area to make your site. When you have finished it and are taking in some money, then you can pay the $8 - $30 a month for the site (to make sure that it works with large numbers of visitors).

CHAPTER 5 - HOW TO LAUNCH AN ONLINE BRANDING PROGRAM THAT REALLY GETS YOU NOTICED.

Launching yourself as an online brand can be really daunting. Especially, if you have just discovered that the sprawling social network medium has more to offer your personal brand than just reunions with old school friends that moved away and you haven't met for years.

How can it be that launching yourself online is the least complex and the most creative of ways to reach out to others with your personal brand, you get a chance to reinvent yourself.

Well orchestrated brands have depth and richness. They are like personalities, in that the best of them are made interesting and beautiful by a unique blend of interesting and beautiful component parts. It is only in the harmony of the whole that the brand lives."
- Steve Yastrow, author Brand Harmony and host of the brand café at www.tompeters.com

Reinventing oneself sounds like a cheesy, schmaltzy concept that not all of us feel the need for, but it really works to differentiate yourself from the regular Facebook geeks and social bugs whose influence is not as wide spread as someone who uses the online world to gain a brand image that will help them achieve their goals.

So, how do you go about launching yourself online and getting and getting noticed for it?

Like we discussed a few times before, if you're online, live, and kicking ass on connective sites then you are....wait for it.....already a brand!

The real question here that should be of more interest to you is how really to get noticed through your online brand. We're talking astronomical proportions of noticeable. Joining Facebook, Twitter, Instagram, Pinterest, and LinkedIn etc. are good ways to exist on the online web as an available entity in the sea of several uniquely characterized entities, but they do not help you branch out magically.

1. Completed profiles

It is always good to have completed profile, may that be on Facebook, Twitter, and LinkedIn. A better completed Linked In profile will help you with job searches. Linked In can suggest better jobs for you the more specifications it has from your profile. People looking to hire you will be pleased with a complete profile. Something they can use as a condensed resume without seeing or talking to you. Think of your Linked in profile as a personal brand image you are projecting. Now pretend you are the employer and view it objectively. What do you see? Do you see gaps in your profile that you would look better with filled up? Linked In is a great place not only to find career opportunities, but also to create great contacts through networking. You can get referrals from past employers and display them on your profile as a show of your experience and past achievements. Employers who are searching for candidates this way always like to see a detailed profile with references and referrals so that they can seriously think about hiring you. This also makes you look more sincere, credible as a candidate and someone who is serious. So, don't ignore the empty spaces in your social media apps, especially if it's Linked In. This will make all the difference in influencing a great firm for an amazing job.

2. Mobile Applications

Target applications that can be downloaded on mobiles also because that is the new 'IN' thing nowadays. Applications that are mobile compatible are preferred because many people go about their business online when they are on the go. Not everyone sits with their laptop or desk top all the time anymore. It's less time consuming and mobiles are in usage 24-7 so you can't knock it unless you try it.

According to a new consensus regarding mobile usage, the percentage of mobile usage and its applications have risen to an amazing 250%. This means more and more people are using their smart phones to connect online with others and this applies on a larger level than just a social aspect.

More statistics show mobile preference to online usage:

- 40% of YouTube videos play from mobiles.

- It is estimated that in 2015 tablets will take over the usage of personal computers and laptops.

- Twitter users are 79% more likely to be online several times during the day through their mobiles.

- Even Yelp searches have increased to 59% through mobiles.

- Pinterest users connect more through mobiles and share 3x more content than general users on laptops and PC's.

- Compared to 4.1% increase in sharing on desktops there is a 7.1% increase in mobile sharing.

Mobile users have accessed Linked In profiles more through their phones than an actual PC or laptop. So, you're first and best bet would be to filter the numerous applications availability on the mobile's App store and kick start your personal brand launchpad through well targeted mobile apps. Facebook, Twitter, Instagram, and LinkedIn are all available in the mobile App stores and can be used easily for greater connectivity with people of interest.

Most of these Apps are free for mobile downloads. So, launching your personal brand will not be an expense ridden deal. You can put your mind to ease. Online personal brand launching has to be the cheapest and easiest way to increase your web influence. You just have to know which buttons to press, literally.

3. Consistency in your messages

Consistency is the road to success. Or at least it leads to success in various aspects of self marketing. Whatever message you're trying to give your target audience through the social media, it has to be consistent in terms of all your profiles. If your Facebook profile gives other s a positive message, your twitter account, and blog account should reflect this image as a standardized message.

If your twitter account shows you as brash and irresponsible in the midst of twitter wars and a perfectly calm and intelligent Facebook, or linked in profile, the audience will not make the connection, the brand image you are trying to project will not gel with the present image.

Consistency is the key in developing those essential connections with others and spreading your message to the rest of the world. If you are consistent others will respond to the continuity of your character online.

4. Internet beside manner- Don't Be an Internet Stalker

Yes, exactly what it says. Don't follow around others obsessively trying to ingrain and an image of yourself.

Patience is a virtue for a good reason. When you launch an online brand, don't expect it to be an immediate success just because you're a natural at socializing. You might have socializing skills up to the maximum, but your internet bed side manner reflects greatly on your online image.

Comments you give on your Facebook and twitter. Pictures you send through Instagram are all influential in image creation and brand launch. If the nature of your Facebook comments is dubious and fake, you might be subject to a certain amount of disdain from your target audience. So, when you create a Facebook profile think about its various aspects and how they will affect you in launching a personal brand.

Just think of your target audience and what facet of your personality you want them to see. Do you want them to see you as a qualified and eloquent person who is responsible? It might not be a great idea to tweet how drunk you got partying and how many times you had to use the bathroom. This probably is not a part of your brand image; keep a separate profile for casual, relaxed banter, which isn't mean to be a part of your personal branding image.

5. Use web analytics for making wise decisions

Creating and launching a brand image that is noticed by millions is ambitious, it is also difficult if you are blinded regarding your target audience and the impact your website is having on those visiting it. This is where web analytics comes in. Website publishers often use this software to know how many people visited their websites, the geographical location of those visiting it and if they visited a link to get to the site.

This can also tell website owners what parts of the website are more popular and whether the website is working properly. You can use this information to make good decisions that will positively affect your personal brand image. You can add more content that certain geographical location users respond more too.

6. The importance of writing articles

Articles are a great way to expand your business. They hang around for years in dental surgeries, hospitals and libraries. They are also free to advertise in, if you go about it intelligently.

The best way to market a new brand is to get your article published in one of the 3500+ magazines out there. It's a great way to advertise a brand and also your personal brand. When you write a 1000 word article detailing your product, or services you are marketing not only your product, website, and services. You are also advertising our personal brand by creating an authentic image that holds integrity. Blogging is more about tapping into the emotions of readers through you views on some subject matter in an expectedly objective manner. And articles require a certain amount of objectivity and integrity. So, this is a good way to lend your brand some credibility.

- You will be marketing yourself with great exposure. Marketing in magazines is a cheaper alternative than using other avenues.

- Magazines are looked upon with confidence by youth and adults alike.

- People have more faith in things magazines say then they do in other publications online, and offline. Any magazine ads are considered more seriously because they aren't treated as some filler material that clutters magazine space.

- It helps that 70% of online purchases are driven through a nudge from magazines featuring fashion, cosmetics, food, and holidays, etc.

- www.ppa.co.uk gives a 3,213 statistic of consumers reading magazines in the UK, reaching about 87% of the population.

- Magazines articles are mostly discussed among family, friends, and talked about on social networks as well. So, that provides you with a good opportunity to reach as many readers as possible.

Now that's some exposure, wouldn't you say? Dan Schawbel writes for both Forbes and Time Magazine.

7. Brand presence

Creating a brand that is 'always present', which is the purpose of good advertising. Adverts target you when you are not hungry. So, that when you are, you will choose that brand, your online brand has to be the same. Find a niche and exploit it.

8. Testimonials

Positive Comments and reviews on your Linked In profile can help you find better opportunities and develop your brand positively. Freelancing communities online thrive on testimonials from clients for better job referrals and invites. It's not surprising that positive testimonials and comments on a Linked In account can help get you better opportunities because the your target audience can trust you credibility if they don't know your professionally, or personally enough to make the judgment based on just your profile alone.

Likewise, testimonials on your website about your content can help increase followers and readers and give you more popularity. Personal branding is after all about gaining positive reviews in many different ways, and having glowing recommendations from your target audience are the best way to convince others of your being different from your competition. Think about it, do you ever buy a cosmetics product without reading reviews from other users and comparing the number of positive reviews to the negative ones?

9. Introvert? No problem

Not all of you who want to create a personal brand are natural born extroverts who have socializing skills up the maximum, but no worries you can still build a strong brand image through social media applications.

Being an introvert doesn't mean you can't be a brand.

Behind a computer, you can be anyone you want. Just because you are quiet and less socially active in your downtime does not mean that you cannot launch a great personal brand that connects with your target audience. It's true that extroverts are more likely to further their brand development much more easily than someone who is nervous about mingling or networking in the physical world.

For those of us who are shy about public speaking, or demonstrative leadership in the tangible world, you need to be a master navigator of social media applications and use them to your advantage. It's good to foster contacts and create a working relationship with your target audience through blogs and social networks. Bolster your confidence through powering your message online. This will help you not only with self esteem, but also will give you more time to strengthen your online presence.

Use your downtime to plan your personal branding strategy and your content. This will help your brand development process because when you launch yourself online, it will be a gradual learning experience and the quicker to start and longer you plan, the more successful your brand will be.

10. Watching out for killer social media mistakes

This helps you marginally reduce chances of social media mistakes that can hurt your brand image. Not all of us are perfect at dealing with the influx of issues that affect us when we start using social media applications for something other than casual friendships and just to keep in touch with family and friends. Just as there are etiquettes of dealing with social media applications, there are also plenty of mistakes you may be making on such networks that hinder your success in achieving that positively known personal brand status. This is not just a lesson in marketing yourself; it's about the image you are producing through all the marketing. Image is what affects your personal brand more than other things.

Social media can be a very powerful tool in personal branding, if you use it right. Someone would say that there aren't any set rules, and this is not a scientific equation. While in some cases I would agree on personal branding not being an exact science, but in certain situations and usage of tools require a more scientific approach from you to achieve that balance, which doesn't over, nor overdo it.

Don't Use the wrong metrics to measure your success

You may feel that because you have about a thousand followers on your twitter, or Facebook account that your personal brand has become a success. Viewer ratings for TV channels and shows decide the future of a show on the channel, some get cancelled early if the viewers and ratings don't increase, but success in social media cannot be measured using the same yard stick. You need to look at your 'following' objectively and decide whether any of the popularity and following online has brought you some form of increased business, or better opportunities in form of an amazing job offer with a reputable firm. If it hasn't than you can't call it success.

Don't use multiple social media applications without a plan

If you're going to use Facebook, twitter and the various other networks without a strategic plan as to how they will impact your personal brand. After all that is why you are trying to create a presence on the online social networks. Find out where your passion lies and how you want it to translate with these social media websites. Don't just aimlessly join a bunch and then never check them regularly. The more such websites you join the more time you will have to spend on updating them and maintaining your target audience's interactions satisfactorily. This can be a hard feat if you don't have the time and are swamped with other things you need to do. So, best to join the ones that 'matter' the most and can give your personal brand an adequate voice.

Don't ignore comments you don't like

Not all of us say all the right things all the time, there will be times when you're blog entry will have supporters and oppositional responses too. You have to deal with them in a patient and controlled way. So, that an angry backlash from you does not to discourage users from reading further content and at the same time you show them that you are appreciating their views as well. Try to respectfully disagree over a difference of opinion, between you and the reader. Remember, you are trying to build a personal brand that gets noticed for its positive aspects and not because you are perceived as arrogant and belligerent when you see a comment that is not respectful, or disagrees with your post. Being graceful and charming will help you win over those naysayers better than being blunt and angry.

Don't use your blog to brag, use it to brand

There are instances where you feel tempted to talk about your achievements, which is commendable as long as it's done tastefully, without sounding completely obnoxious and turning people 'off' from your image online. There is a fine line between talking about achievement in the flow of things and just bragging about yourself on your blog. We all have seen countless blogs and twitter accounts that give show an obnoxious host and either we remember them for being horribly arrogant, or we just don't remember them at all, neither a good option if you are trying to get your personal brand high up among others.

Don't use your professional social media account as a personal one

This point has been brought up before in the book, but simply cannot be emphasized enough. It's 'never' a good idea to divulge personal tweets, or Facebook statuses that can be perceived as negative. So, if you got drunk and strung as high as a flag you need not use your professional social media account to alert the mass of followers who view you as this together and professional personal brand. A personal brand image can easily be affected by this negatively.

Don't get involved in controversial discussions

Everyone has personal beliefs that are different and 'personal' from each other and sometimes other people might not understand when you get involved in twitter, or Facebook wars that focus on certain political and controversial subjects that give some definitive position from your side, something that if a majority of people agree with might get you a positive over flow of followers and otherwise a negative influx of comments and shunning by previously content target audience.

Don't try to capitalize on certain holidays

Large companies like AT&T got into trouble when they tried to evoke emotions and capitalize on the events of 9/11. They were shamed by an outpouring of outrage over this. So, it is always advised not to try and create business opportunities that may obtrusively make you seem opportunistic, and show that you disrespect emotions, and issues surrounding the incident. If you want to talk about it respectfully, you can post a message on your website, etc. politely condemning the destruction and loss of life, but don't go overboard as viewer emotions tend to be sensitive regarding such dates.

Don't be inactive for long periods

Being inactive on Facebook and other social media networks will only reduce your following and make you seem in active and uninteresting. Regularly update your statuses online and make sure when you are not posting your next article you have some interesting links, thoughts and videos to share with others to keep the interest of viewers. The many personal brands emerging and several distracting social media applications also prompt a certain lowered attention span. It's common for us to lose interest in someone who is not regularly updating their websites and social media accounts no matter how authentic and interesting their personal brand image might be.

Don't proclaim to know everything about a social media application

Even Facebook regularly changes its user settings and inside applications. You should keep an eye on these changes and see if they can positively affect your personal brand. Don't be stuck in the last year. With increasing web applications and user needs, such social media applications are always evolving and making their service better and more customized for our use. Personal branding wise they can be astronomical in helping you get a leg up on the competition.

Don't pass the world by, online

Knowing what your competitors are doing that makes them different, or keeping up with the latest post by someone with a similar personal brand, is not cheating. There is nothing wrong with giving reference to someone else's work, post, or words as long as you provide the source and don't take credit for it. Referencing someone is the ultimate compliment.

Don't pass on your work to social media bots

Avoid trying to seem like a robot by not letting a 'bot' take care of your tweets and programming them as such. News is always random and comes when you least expect it, if you allow your tweets to be pre-programmed you may look out of touch when some new topic of discussion emerges.

Don't give unauthentic apologies

That's right, everyone makes mistakes with things they say, or aren't sensitive about the viewers views in some way, but you can make it right by apologizing. Essentially just saying 'sorry' helps and keeping it brief is even better. People will recognize you are a human and made a genuine error in judgment. Don't appear averse to apologizing in your message to others and make it seem as if you are doing your readers and followers a favor.

Don't offer candid advice on things you know nothing about

It's always of paramount importance to make sure you know what you are talking about before you make a post anywhere and especially on topics that can be controversial and can trigger negative inflow of reviews by readers. Like tweets and content that can be considered sexist in some way, or raises questions on sexual orientation, or teen suicide issues, unless you are some expert with a doctorate. Remember everyone has personal views, but is this is something that is not relative to your personal brand image and can be negatively damaging to your brand, then don't make the mistake of posting.

Don't let the wrong people run your social media accounts

It's possible you may not have enough time to visit and update all your social media accounts, especially if you have scores of followers and comments that you need to attend to. It may seem like a good idea to contract this responsibility to someone else like an employee, a co worker, etc. While, there is nothing wrong with do so, if the employee, or whoever you employee for this purpose gets you good results. There have been incidents however, where inappropriate, or damaging tweets and statuses have been posted and these in turn have negatively impacted your personal brand image. So, if you are still going to contract someone for these responsibilities make sure you know what they are doing, and make certain that they are on board with what your brand is all about. They should know what will negatively and positively affect your personal brand.

11. Personal Branding Success stories

"Branding demands commitment; commitment to continual re-invention; striking chords with people to stir their emotions; and commitment to imagination. It is easy to be cynical about such things, much harder to be successful."

- Sir Richard Branson, CEO Virgin.

Everyone has people that inspire them to follow their dreams and ambitions and my book came to fruition no differently. There are several personal branding gurus that I admire and who have done a lot for online personal branding. Their achievements make everything in this book probable and easy. They have a huge online following and are bestselling authors of personal branding topics.

Dan Schawbel

You may have noticed most of the quotes in my book are from him. He is the young face of personal branding and author of two bestselling books like 'Me 2.0- four steps to building your future' and 'Promote yourself- The new rules for career success' . He is personal branding guru that contributes to both Time Magazine and Forbes Magazine. That in itself is amazing right? But that's not all. He is also the managing partner of Millennial Branding, which is a Generation Y research and consulting firm.

This man has appeared on several media outlets such as the Today show and NBC and spoke at Universal, McGraw Hill, Harvard business school, etc. He has a strong following due to perseverance and constant innovation in his field. His personal branding success is an inspiration to all of us who are struggling to find that same success. His blogs are influential and uplifting with staunch focus on various personal branding concepts.

William Arruda

Is the global personal branding expert who has been a much sought after expert on topics of personal branding, motivation, and social media. He is the founder of 'Reach' the personal branding consultant firm online that provides brand trained brand strategists that can help build powerful personal brands. William Arruda is someone who works with the world's strongest brands like IBM, Lotus, Cisco, American Express, Adobe, etc. He is a force to reckon with when it comes to matters of personal branding. He has delivered many talks and presentations regarding the subject, speaking passionately from his vast experience. He is also an author and has a blog dedicated to personal branding.

"William Arruda is one of the most passionate and enthusiastic presenters I have ever worked with. He delivered a dynamic, authentic, humorous and most importantly insightful presentation to our team. Personal branding for William is a way of life ... and that shows! I am personally still amazed at his impact days after having heard him speak. I recommend him to any organization that seeks to invigorate, motivate and engage their management teams." – Jane Swift, Director, Executive Network, British Telecom says.

J.W. Dicks

Has designed some of the most campaigns of marketing business and is also an author of bestselling personal branding book 'Celebrity Branding You'. His book talks about how to increase your business through personal branding. Taken from www.JWDicks.com/About - "A printer for instance can change their position from "printer" to "trusted expert advisor on using print to build business". An office cleaning company can become an expert at "creating environmentally safe work space". A vacation home real estate agent can become the "expert in vacation experiences". While these are just a few short examples they each show you how a change of position can elevate your status in the minds of prospects that is different from all of the others in that market competing for the same prospect."

This man has helped hundreds of people achieve the bestselling author status and has shown others how to achieve that 'celebrity expert' status in their own niche. It is truly inspiring to see what this man has done to help others achieve their dreams and ambitions.

These men are amazing at what they do and have achieved personal branding at its greatest. They are true inspirations to all of us who seek to become a household name in our fields.

CONCLUSION

'A great brand is a story that's never completely told. A brand is a metaphorical story that connects with something very deep – a fundamental appreciation of mythology. Stories create the emotional context people need to locate themselves in a larger experience.'

- Scott Bedbury - Nike, Starbucks

In conclusion it's hard to say that everything in this book will crush your competition and give you your dream, but this book gives the best of the best advice available on online personal branding. The right decisions in a personal brand development can give you a brand image that can live and grow independently for years, profitable in many positive ways to you. And many of us would like to get their sooner rather than later, but alas, personal branding is not a five minute roller coaster ride that you can expect to be done within a few snap decisions.

Personal branding, if we have learned anything is an ongoing, learning curve that is never over. You need to have patience to deal with the hurdles and the evolving web applications that may seem to have become more and more complicated. It's true that a person fears the unknown. Once you have educated yourself with the latest ongoing changes and keep track of new applications that come out of nowhere and capture the imagination of millions on the World Wide Web, you will be set to rule your own niche.

There are always failures and wins that come with challenges and online personal brand building is no exception to this rule. Maybe, it is more applicable in this case, despite everything you do to avoid failure, there will be someone who has a better vision to your field and can build a stronger personal brand than you. The key is to never give up. These are times of uncertainty with fluctuating economies, job markets, and consumer loyalties. So, prepare to be patient and learn with your mistakes as you rise to the top with a successful brand. You can only rise to the top if you persevere as many others have triumph in their chosen endeavors.

Sources

www.JWDicks.com/About

www.Careerfolk.com

http://www.dummies.com.

www.techforluddites.com

www.ppa.co.uk

http://www.garyhyman.com/5-easy-steps-to-build-an-effective-social-media-content-strategy/

www.reachcc.com

www.lifeworkalliance.com/

http://danschawbel.com/blog/book-trailer-why-millennials-matter/

www.dailyblogtips.com

I hope you have enjoyed The Branding Book and will implement several of the strategies in these pages to make your online life more profitable. Chances are it has taken you a couple of days to work through this book. In that time, the online world has altered in a million different ways.

Keep up to date with all the changes at:

www.thebrandingbook.co.uk